Yes we can read™

The one-to-one reading scheme
for learners from 8 to 80

Written by Libby Coleman & Nick Ainley

Gate
HOUSE

Yes we can read
Copyright © Libby Coleman & Nick Ainley 2010

Art Concept: Libby Coleman
Picture Researcher: Claudia Tate
Design: Marcus Tate & Nick Ainley
All images: Marcus Tate, Dreamstime.com, Fotolia.com, Istock.com, Shutterstock.com
Cover design: Cornerstone Design & Marketing
Editor: Catherine White

ISBN: 978-1-84231-075-5

First published in England in 2010 by Gatehouse Media Limited. Reprinted in 2011, 2014 and 2017.

British Library CIP Data:
A catalogue record for this book is available from the British Library.

Printed and bound in Great Britain by Printfine Limited.

Copies of *Yes we can read* can be ordered from:

Gatehouse Media Limited
PO Box 965
Warrington
WA4 9DE

Phone: +44 (0)1925 267778
Email: info@gatehousebooks.com
Online: www.gatehousebooks.com

The *Yes we can read* website is at: www.yeswecanread.co.uk

This book belongs to the Learner:

....

INTRODUCTION FOR THE COACH

To be a coach you do not require any training. Anyone who can read will successfully coach a relative, friend or neighbour to read fluently, using this one-to-one coaching method.
Just follow the simple, jargon-free coach instructions.

Yes we can read is aimed at people from 8 to 80 with limited or no reading skills.
Few people are unable to read anything at all. However it is essential that you start right at the beginning of *Yes we can read*.
This will enable you to find and remove the obstacles your learner has, in order to be able to read fluently and for meaning.
It will also give your learner confidence right from the start.

If for any reason you have to drop out of coaching, another coach can take over seamlessly, as you will have ticked every step of progress and underlined any problems your learner needs addressing.

Read the general guidance notes before you start and the instructions on the left-hand page before each session.

It works! Yes we can read!

Coach: General Guidance

Encouragement and praise
Always approach every session in a relaxed, friendly and can-do way, so that your learner will feel confident and positive.

Always show your learner how proud and pleased you are with every success, no matter how small.

Reassure your learner that a reading problem, in spite of what anyone says, has nothing to do with intelligence. Some of the cleverest people are dyslexic or have other reading problems - see the list near the back of the book to find the names of people your learner has heard of.

Reassure your learner that you will maintain confidentiality!

Covering the whole course
Every bit of the course must be covered from the beginning of
Yes we can read. If your learner knows, for example, the letter-sounds, then you will work through them anyway - it will be a great opportunity for gaining ticks and confidence. It will also enable you to find and remove the obstacles your learner has, in order to be able to read fluently and for meaning.

Time and number of sessions
Settle into a routine that suits you both, such as half an hour each time, several times a week. If your learner has serious concentration problems it is better if you work together for 20 minutes every day. Your rate of progress will vary: sometimes you might cover two learner pages in one session, sometimes only half a page.

Coach instructions
Read the coach instructions (left-hand pages) before each session.

Marking
Put a tick to mark and celebrate every correct small step, but if your learner has made a slip, underline in pencil - crosses can often be associated with failure at school.

Your learner can make these marks, but it's better if they concentrate on the learning process and you put in the ticks and underlines.

Both of you should be relaxed, be confident and have fun . . .

Repeating exercises
Repeat any exercise more often than suggested whenever you feel this is appropriate for your learner.

Going back
If your learner repeatedly falters over something learned a while ago, you can always break off and re-coach the relevant learning page before returning to where you broke off.

Letter-sounds (phonic sounds)
Use the letter-sounds - **not their alphabet names!** - throughout your reading adventure and speak the sounds soft and short.
Practise the letter-sounds on your own before you start coaching, pretending to yourself to stutter over the words on the alphabet page. This method is explained in detail on the relevant coach pages.

Look Write Say for exceptions and your learner's difficult words
Some everyday words in the English language don't follow any pattern and just have to be learned. You will use the *Look Write Say* method, which is explained in detail on the relevant coach pages.
You will also use this method for any words your learner finds difficult.

Concentration
Some days your learner may have good concentration, on others not. This may depend on the time of day, or the weather, or other factors in your learner's life. When you notice your learner is losing concentration, just end the session after briefly practising a difficult letter or word.

Punctuation marks
When your learner asks you about particular punctuation marks, explain their purpose in your own words.

Regional accents
It is helpful if the coach and learner have similar regional accents.

. . . and remember that your learner will become a fluent reader.

Learner and Coach start their reading adventure...

Coach

Pictures

Approach your sessions in a relaxed, friendly and can-do way,
so that your learner will always feel confident and positive.

Look at the book together. Read the title with your learner.
Make sure they repeat and know the title of the book.
You are now ready to start your adventure together.

Together look at the photos on the learner's page opposite.
Point to each image and ask your learner just to name the image.
What's that?.... it's an apple,   it's a queen,   it's a snake   etc.
Once your learner can name all the objects, and all the images are
fixed in their mind, you can move on to the next page.

	apple	bat + ball	cat	duck
egg	flower	girl	hat	insect
	jam jar	king	leg	mouth
	nail	orange	pan	queen
rainbow	snake	tree	umbrella	vans
	worm	kiss	yo-yo	zip

Before the next session
practise saying the letter-sounds on your own, pretending to stutter:
a a a apple,   b b b bat and ball,   c c c cat,   etc.
Make the sounds soft and short
To pronounce the letter **x**, which is the exception, say the word **kiss** softly
and quickly, **ks**.
Your learner will learn **only the sound** of each letter, **not the name**,
so **not ay, bee, cee, etc.**

(This is the only time you will have to do preparation beforehand.)

Coach

Just to remind you:
Before you start this session with your learner, practise saying the letter-sounds on your own, pretending to stutter:
a a a apple,   b b b bat and ball,   c c c cat,   etc.
Make the sounds soft and short
To pronounce the letter **x** say the word **kiss** softly and quickly, **ks**.
Your learner will learn **only the sound** of each letter, **not the name,** so **not ay, bee, cee, etc.**

> **Your learner does not need to know the names of each letter - i.e. ay, bee, cee etc. - in order to learn to read.**

Letter-sounds

Look at each photo on pages 14 and 15 and ask your learner to name the image. Then move your finger to the letter-sound next to it.

Make the sounds soft and short as you say

a... apple... a,   b... bat and ball... b,   c... cat... c,   etc.

For each photo + letter, follow the line of the letter with your own finger while saying the sound of the letter.
Then ask your learner to do the same.

Discover together that the photos are shaped like the letters!

Remember that to pronounce the letter **x** say the word **kiss** softly and quickly, **ks,**
and point out to your learner: that is why we put x x x for kisses.

Point out that the letters **c** and **k** make the same sound.

If your learner hesitates, or reads a letter-sound incorrectly, wait four seconds and then give the correct letter-sound in a neutral voice.

If some letters still present difficulties after you have worked through pages 14 and 15, then the page opposite gives you a variety of tips for dealing with these difficult letters.

Coach

Tips for dealing with your learner's difficult letters

When you know what your learner's difficult letters are, you have an opportunity for fun in future sessions.
Be as creative as you like - discover what works best for you both.

Try some of these tips . . .

Sing the problem letter to a well-known tune like Happy Birthday "d-d-d-d-d-d, d-d-d-d-d-d, d-d-d-d-dear-duck, d-d-d-d to you."

Make the shape of the letter with your hands or bodies.

Write the problem letter on paper, or in the earth or sand.

Play "I spy, with my squinty eye, a word beginning with d."

Put on the table in front of you a bat and ball facing 'the b way' or a toy duck facing 'the d way'.

Call the problem letter your 'special letter' and say for instance, "Quick, quick, let's practise reading our special letter q quickly."

Point at the letter and ask your learner to whisper its letter sound, and then to say it louder, and louder!

Send your learner a letter or postcard with the letter and its corresponding picture.

Use any of these ideas for any problem words later on.

(One of our younger learners horrified his coach by displaying a tattoo of his problem letters on his forearm. It was a transfer and washed off after a week, but from then on qu was welcomed with glee by the ten-year-old boy.)

If your learner has difficulty repeating some of the letter-sounds you make, you should arrange for a hearing test to check for hearing difficulties.

If your learner appears to have difficulty seeing the letters clearly, perhaps holding the book closer or further away, you should arrange for an eyesight check.

 a  b  c

 d  e

f g h

 i  j

k  l  m

n n  o o p p

q r r

s s t u

v v w w

x x y z z

Coach

Letter-sounds practice

Your learner may find it easier if one of you covers the next letters with your hand or a piece of card.

The letter-sounds your learner knows can be ticked by one of you.

If your learner hesitates or reads a letter-sound incorrectly, wait four seconds and then, in a neutral voice, give the correct letter-sound. After your learner has repeated the letter-sound correctly, underline it and move on.

If your learner has struggled with several letter-sounds, turn back and work through pages 14 and 15 again.

Two ticks are needed for each letter-sound. The ticks must be earned on different days, so repeat this learning page at the start of your next session.

After all (or nearly all) of the letter-sounds have been ticked twice, move on to the next page.

If there are still a few problem letter-sounds, practise them at the beginning of each session -
use some of the **Tips** on page 13, or make up your own.

Don't worry! You won't go wrong.
Your learner will tell you what works and what doesn't.

Tip

Sit at a table, and make sure that you have good light.

Having a glass of water to sip and peppermints to suck can help your concentration.

Keep a couple of pencils handy, and a sheet of spare paper.

Learner read:

✓   ✓

s

a

t

i

p

n

c

k

e

h

r

m

g

o

q

u

l

f

b

j

z

w

v

d

y

x

Coach

Two-letter words

Read each word in the list to your learner:
slide your finger along under the word and
say the letter-sounds without stopping between the letters,
smoothly sliding from one sound into the next.

Then ask your learner to repeat each word after you:

coach:	**a..m am**	learner:	**a..m am**	then
coach:	**a..n an**	learner:	**a..n an**	then
coach:	**a..t at**	learner:	**a..t at**	etc.

Next, ask your learner to read the words in the list on their own -
each word your learner reads correctly can be ticked.

If your learner reads a word incorrectly, or hesitates, wait four
seconds and then, in a neutral voice, say the letter-sounds without
stopping between the letters and then the whole word,
e.g. **o..x ox**

After your learner has repeated the word correctly, underline it and
move on.

After your learner has tried all the words, coach
any underlined words.

Repeat this learning page at the start of your next session.

Share your learner's excitement about reading real words,
and when your learner has read all the words twice, write
your learner's name in at the bottom of the page
- this is an opportunity for celebration.

Coach read each word first, and ask your learner to repeat it.

Next, ask your learner to read them all without prompting.

✓   ✓

am

an

at

ax

ex

if

in

is

it

on

op

ox

up

us

.... can read words!

Coach

Two-letter words practice

Ask your learner to read each phrase and
give every correct phrase a tick.

If your learner reads a word incorrectly, or hesitates, wait four
seconds, and then in a neutral voice say the word correctly.
When your learner has repeated the word correctly, underline it and
move on.

After your learner has tried all the words, coach
any underlined words.

If your learner has struggled with several new words, turn back and
work through the learning page again.

When every phrase has been ticked twice, remember to
write in your learner's name.

Tip

> Together think of rude words that 'you shouldn't normally use'
> which begin with letter-sounds your learner has difficulty with.
> "Bum starts with **b**" is a good example for a younger learner...
> You will be surprised how motivating this is. It also helps to
> develop reading for meaning: an older male learner said,
> "Pity I find **p** and **q** hard - **b** and **f** would have been more fun."

Learner read:

✓   ✓

on on on

in on it

on at us

it is up

if it is on

it is an ax

it is an ox

Coach

Three-letter words

As before, read each word in the list to your learner:
slide your finger along under the word and
say the letter-sounds without stopping between the letters,
smoothly sliding from one sound into the next.

Then ask your learner to repeat the words after you:

coach:	**c..a..n**	**can**	learner:	**c..a..n**	**can**	then
coach:	**d..o..g**	**dog**	learner:	**d..o..g**	**dog**	then
coach:	**y..e..s**	**yes**	learner:	**y..e..s**	**yes**	etc.

Next ask your learner to read all the words in the list on their own.
Tick the words your learner reads correctly.

If your learner reads a word incorrectly, or hesitates, wait four
seconds and then, in a neutral voice, say the letter-sounds, sliding
into each other and then the whole word,
e.g. **r..a..t   rat**

After your learner has repeated the word correctly, underline it and
move on.

After your learner has tried all the words, coach
any underlined words.

Repeat this learning page at the start of your next session.

When your learner has read all the words twice, write your learner's
name in at the bottom of the page to celebrate.

Tip

> Tell your learner that they are now able to read over 400 words!
> These include the word for a Chinese cooking pan and the
> name of a one-time king of Albania! Hot!

Coach read each word, then ask your learner to read it to you.

Next, ask your learner to read them all out without prompting.

✓ ✓

can

dog

yes

hit

wax

am

rat

gun

win

dot

pan

bat

let

if

not

can

sip

vet

.... **can read lots of words!**

Coach

the

Read the three words **the** to your learner and ask your learner to repeat it each time.

Then ask your learner to read each line in the list.

Give every correct pair of words a tick.

If your learner reads a word incorrectly, or hesitates, wait four seconds and then, in a neutral voice, say the two words correctly, e.g. **the rat**

After your learner has repeated the two words correctly, underline them and move on.

After your learner has tried all the words, coach any underlined words.

Repeat this learning page at the start of your next session.

Coach read:

the

Coach read each word, and then learner:

the   the   the

Learner read:

✓   ✓

the top

the can

the dog

the hat

the zip

the wax

the lot

the rat

the fin

the mat

the gun

the jam

the bat

the pan

the hip

Coach

phrases with **three-letter words**

If all the words are right, tick the phrase.

If your learner misreads a word, or hesitates, wait four seconds then say the word correctly in a neutral voice. After your learner has repeated the word correctly, underline it and move on.

After your learner has tried all the phrases, coach any underlined words.

When your learner has correctly read all the phrases twice, write your learner's name in at the bottom of the page
- this is another opportunity for celebration.

Tip

Bring sweets or other treats for your learner, and don't hand them over until they have read the name on the packet.
One of our learners had difficulty with **qu**, and her coach managed to find a snack that began with **qu**.

Learner read:

tick   tick

the man can pat a cat

the man can pat a dog

let the vet get a pig

the vet can get a pig

win a tin cup

win a big tin cup

the fox sat on a big log

an ox let a fox run

the red hen is in a hut

the red fox met a red hen

the man has a big nut

a fat rat sat on a mat

a bad fat rat sat on a bat

.... **can read better.**

Coach

th

In the first row, put your finger under each word and read it and ask your learner to read it to you.

In the second row, ask your learner to put their finger under each word and read it to you, without prompting from you.

If your learner misreads a word, or hesitates, wait four seconds then say the word correctly in a neutral voice. After your learner has repeated the word correctly, underline it and move on along the row.

After your learner has tried all the words, coach any underlined words.

Then work along this row a second time.

Then ask your learner to read each sentence. (Capital letters will be taught shortly.)

Tick each sentence when your learner has read it through correctly without hesitation.

If your learner misreads a word, correct it, underline, and move on.

After your learner has tried all the sentences, coach any underlined words.

Repeat this page at the start of your next session.

Coach read each word, then learner read it:

the   then   this   that   thin

Learner read:

✓✓   ✓✓   ✓✓   ✓✓   ✓✓
    this   that   then   the   thin

Learner read sentences:

tick   tick

this cat sat on that rat.

then that rat bit this cat.

this thin pig is in the wet mud.

then that thin pig is wet.

the thin man sat on the fat dog.

then the fat dog sat on the thin man.

that is the thin hen.

then that thin hen can get fat.

this is the bat that bit the man.

that is the bat that bit the dog.

Yes, ... can read sentences.

Coach

Plurals

Tell your learner: **s** at the end of a word can mean **more than one**.

Ask your learner to read the words. Tick correct words.

If your learner misreads a word, or hesitates, wait four seconds then say the word correctly in a neutral voice. After your learner has repeated the word correctly, underline it and move on.

After your learner has tried all the words, coach any underlined words.

At least two ticks need to be earned, on different days, so repeat this learning page at the start of your next session.

Learner read:

    ✓   ✓

cats

bat

bats

pig

pigs

ram

rams

pet

pets

dog

dogs

hug

hugs

sob

sobs

bed

beds

tins

lots

Coach

reading practice

If all the words are right, tick the sentence.

If your learner misreads a word, or hesitates, wait four seconds then say the word correctly in a neutral voice. After your learner has repeated the word correctly, underline it and move on.

After your learner has tried all the sentences, coach any underlined words.

When every sentence has been ticked twice, remember to write in your learner's name.

Learner read:

tick   tick

this man has ten cats and ten pups.

that man sits on his bed with the cats.

this man lets his pups sit on the mats.

that man fed the six thin pups.

this man has zits on his lip.

that man hits his dog and that man is bad.

this man on the bus has six cats in a box.

that man has six pigs and ten hens.

this man has bats in his hut.

that man has six bugs as pets.

Yes, ... can read sentences.

Coach

Capital Letters

Starting with **A**, put your finger under each capital letter and say its letter-sound, short and soft.
Ask your learner to say the letter-sound after you.
Remember you do not use the letter name, i.e. ay, bee, cee.

When you've done all 26, ask your learner to put their finger under each capital letter and say its letter-sound to you.
Tick each correct one on its left side.

Then ask your learner to go through all the capital letters again, this time randomly. Put another tick every time your learner says the letter-sound correctly without prompting from you, until each letter has at least three ticks.

If your learner has particular difficulty with one of the capital letter-sounds, ask your learner to trace round the shape with a finger, or write over it repeatedly in pencil . . .

. . . if your learner traces the **B**, show them
      how **B** is like a bat next to two balls on top of each other.

. . . if your learner traces the **D**, point out
      how capital **D** is the other way round to the small **d**.

A   B   C   D   E

F   G   H   I   J

K   L   M   N   O

P   Qu   R   S   T

U   V   W   X   Y

Z

Coach

Capital Letters practice

If all the words are right, tick the sentence.

If your learner misreads a word, or hesitates, wait four seconds then say the word correctly in a neutral voice. After your learner has repeated the word correctly, underline it and move on.

After your learner has tried all the sentences, coach any underlined words.

When every sentence has been ticked twice, remember to write in your learner's name.

Learner read:

tick   tick

Mum, Al and Ed met Dan the man.

Dan the man met Zog the dog.

Zog the dog met Hat the rat.

Hat the rat met Sam the ram.

Sam the ram met Pat the cat.

Pat the cat met Jen the hen.

Jen the hen met Nat the bat.

Nat the bat met Big the pig.

Big the pig met Rox the fox.

Rox the fox met Mum, Al and Ed.

Well done .... !

Coach

more **Capital Letters** practice

If all the words are right, tick the sentence.

If your learner misreads a word, or hesitates, wait four seconds then say the word correctly in a neutral voice. After your learner has repeated the word correctly, underline it and move on.

After your learner has tried all the sentences, coach any underlined words.

When your learner knows all the capital letters explain that when the capital letter **I** is on its own it is said like its letter name, not its sound.

Coach explain:

"*When you see **I** on its own, it is said **eye**.*"

Learner read:

tick   tick

Dan the Dad has hens.

Yes Dan the Dad has hens.

Vic the Dad is big.

Yes Vic the Dad is big.

Ken the Dad has cats.

Yes Ken the Dad has cats.

Bob the Dad is fat.

Yes Bob the Dad is fat.

Quin the Dad has dogs.

Yes Quin the Dad has dogs.

Len the Dad has a hat.

Yes Len the Dad has a hat.

Ted the Dad has pups.

Pups.

Yes Ted the Dad has pups.

Will the Dad has fun.

Fun.

Yes Will the Dad has fun.

Good work ....

Coach

sh

Tell your learner:
when **s** and **h** appear together, they make a new sound - **sh**.

At the top of the learner's page, put your finger under each word and read it, then ask your learner to read it to you.

In the next part, ask your learner to put their finger under each word and read it to you.

If your learner misreads a word, or hesitates, wait four seconds then say the word correctly in a neutral voice. After your learner has repeated the word correctly, underline it and move on.

After your learner has tried all the words, coach any underlined words.

Then work through this part a second time.

Ask your learner to read each sentence.
If all the words are right, tick the sentence.
Underline any incorrect words as usual.

After your learner has tried all the sentences, coach any underlined words.

Repeat this page at the start of your next session.

When every sentence has been ticked twice, remember to write in your learner's name.

Coach read each word, then learner read it:

sh	shut	shed	sh	mash	cash
sh	shop	sh	rash	fish	dish

Learner read:

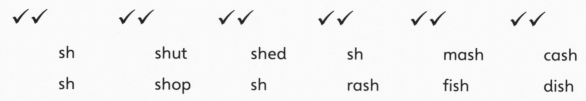

sh	shut	shed	sh	mash	cash
sh	shop	sh	rash	fish	dish

Learner read sentences:

tick   tick

The ship is big. Yes, that ship is a big ship.

The fish from that ship is in the shop.

I wish I had a bit of fish.

Rush to the shop and get fish.

Get the fish with this cash.

In this dish is the fish-shop fish,

and the mash is in that big dish.

The fish shop is shut.

Is the cash in the fish shop?

No, the cash is not in the shop,

but Sam has got a lot of dosh in his shed.

Gosh .... !

Coach

ck

Tell your learner:
when **c** and **k** appear together, they make just one sound.

At the top of the learner's page, put your finger under each word and read it, then ask your learner to read it to you.

In the next part, ask your learner to put their finger under each word and read it to you.

If your learner misreads a word, or hesitates, wait four seconds then say the word correctly in a neutral voice. After your learner has repeated the word correctly, underline it and move on.

After your learner has tried all the words, coach any underlined words.

Then work through this part a second time.

Ask your learner to read each sentence.
If all the words are right, tick the sentence.
Underline any incorrect words as usual.

After your learner has tried all the sentences, coach any underlined words.

Repeat this page at the start of your next session.

When every sentence has been ticked twice, remember to write in your learner's name.

Coach read each word, then learner read it:

sack	nick	hacks	buck	thick	shocks
ticks	jack	muck	shacks	back	dock

Learner read:

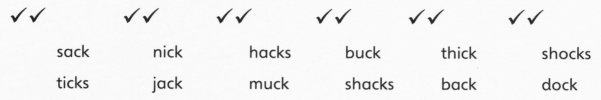

sack	nick	hacks	buck	thick	shocks
ticks	jack	muck	shacks	back	dock

Learner read sentences:

tick   tick

I got a tick, and a pat on the back.

Jack is off sick with a rick in his neck.

Lock up the shop with the cash in it.

Pick up the logs at the back of the shed.

The sun is hot on the deck of this ship.

Mick is that man with the big sack.

With luck, Mick will get that fat fox.

Mick did get it, and the fox is in the sack,

and this duck is in luck.

Yes, ... can read.

Coach

Look Write Say

Everyday words that **don't follow easy rules**
have to be learned by the *Look Write Say* method.

In the top line, point at any word and read it, then ask your learner
to read the word to you.
Don't read the letters separately - **say the whole word** - because
your learner is **MEMORISING the SHAPE of the WHOLE WORD**.

Make sure you cover each word at least twice.

Ask your learner to read you the words in the next section, unprompted.
Tick correct words, otherwise wait four seconds and say
the word correctly, then underline it.

Coach any underlined words.

> If your learner still has difficulty with a word, write it on a piece
>
> of spare paper, saying the word as you write.
>
> Then ask your learner to copy your word, up to ten times,
>
> saying the word as they are writing it.
>
>
> **This is a useful technique for any word**
>
> **your learner struggles with, now or later.**

Ask your learner to read each sentence to you, then either tick it
or correct any misread words and underline them.

After your learner has tried all the sentences, coach
any underlined words.

Repeat this page at the start of your next session.

Coach read each word, then learner read it:

he   my   here   are   one   said

Learner read:

✓ ✓   ✓ ✓   ✓ ✓

he   here   said

one   are   my

Learner read sentences:

tick   tick

Mick said, here is my cat.

And here is a rat, I said.

My big cat will kill that rat, he said.

One of my pigs is in the pig pen,

and the hens are in the pig pen.

Hens? In the pig pen? said my mum.

One hen sat on my lap, and a fat one sat on my hat.

That one is fat, it is the end of my hat!

Yes, ... can read.

Coach

ch

Tell your learner:
when **c** and **h** appear together, they make just one sound - **ch**.

At the top of the learner's page, put your finger under each word and read it, then ask your learner to read it to you.

In the next part, ask your learner to put their finger under each word and read it to you.

If your learner misreads a word, or hesitates, wait four seconds then say the word correctly in a neutral voice. After your learner has repeated the word correctly, underline it and move on.

After your learner has tried all the words, coach any underlined words.

Then work through this part a second time.

Ask your learner to read each sentence.
If all the words are right, tick the sentence.
Underline any incorrect words as usual.

After your learner has tried all the sentences, coach any underlined words.

Repeat this page at the start of your next session.

When every sentence has been ticked twice, remember to write in your learner's name.

Coach read each word, then learner read it:

chop	chips	check	much	chat	chess	tich
chocs	chin	chick	chuck	chill	such	rich

Learner read:

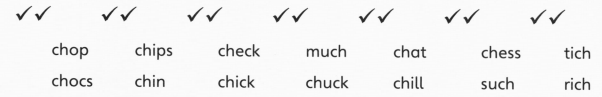

chop	chips	check	much	chat	chess	tich
chocs	chin	chick	chuck	chill	such	rich

Learner read sentences:

tick   tick

The hen and the chicks said chuck chuck-chuck.

Chuck-chuck chuck said the hen and the chicks.

Get chops at that shop.

Chops at the shop?

Yes, I said, get chops at that shop.

This rich man has lots of cash.

This big fat man - is he rich?

Yes, he is such a rich man.

Check the cash in the box

at the back of the shop, he said.

Yes, I said, I will check the box.

Yes, ... can read.

Reading for Fun

> Coach and learner have a go at these tongue twisters:
>
> Chop shops stock chops, chop shops stock chops.
>
> Sam's shop stocks short socks, Sam's shop stocks short socks.

Coach

qu

Tell your learner:
when **q** and **u** appear together, they make just one sound - **qu**.

At the top of the learner's page, put your finger under each word and read it, then ask your learner to read it to you.

In the next part, ask your learner to put their finger under each word and read it to you.

If your learner misreads a word, or hesitates, wait four seconds then say the word correctly in a neutral voice. After your learner has repeated the word correctly, underline it and move on.

After your learner has tried all the words, coach any underlined words.

Then work through this part a second time.

Ask your learner to read each sentence.
If all the words are right, tick the sentence.
Underline any incorrect words as usual.

After your learner has tried all the sentences, coach any underlined words.

Repeat this page at the start of your next session.

Coach read each word, then learner read it:

quick   quack   quit   quiff   quiz   quick   quid

Learner read:

✓✓   ✓✓   ✓✓   ✓✓   ✓✓   ✓✓   ✓✓

quick   quack   quit   quiff   quiz   quick   quid

Learner read sentences:

tick   tick

This duck said quack quack-quack.

Quack-quack quack said the duck.

Is the fox quick?

Yes, the fox is quick

but the hen is quick,

and this man with the gun is quick.

I quit this quiz,

said the man with the big quiff.

Yes, ... can read.

Reading for Fun

Coach and learner have a go at this tongue twister:

Quick kiss, quick kiss, quick kiss, quick kiss, quick kiss.

Coach

reading practice

Ask your learner to read each of these new sentences.
If all the words are right, tick the sentence.

If your learner misreads a word, or hesitates, wait four seconds
then say the word correctly in a neutral voice. After your learner
has repeated the word correctly, underline it and move on.

After your learner has tried all the sentences, coach
any underlined words.

When every sentence has been ticked twice, remember to
write in your learner's name.

Tip

Never worry about going back to revise an earlier page if your
learner has forgotten particular letter-sounds or words.
(The contents are listed at the front of the book.)
One of our youngest learners said, "My mum is proud of me
when I show her how far we have got. But I don't mind
going back sometimes - it makes me feel safe."

Learner read:

tick   tick

The red hen has one chick.

Pick up the pen and the big pad.

Sam has a sick dog, said my dad.

Pick up the sick dog.

Pick up the dog sick?

No! Pick up the sick dog!

The eggs are in the big pan. It is hot.

That chap has one of my six pups.

He is at the shop to get a chop.

The rich man with the big ship is here.

Here is his big ship. It is a quick ship.

The hen and the chick are not here, I said.

Yes I can read, and Pam can read, I said.

I quit.

.... **can read a lot.**

Coach

Blending

Before starting with your learner,
get yourself in the mood for blending consonants together by
saying to yourself - slowly and luxuriously - **slip slide blend**

  b slides into **l**,
    l slides into **e**,
      e slides into **n**,
        n slides into **d**,
making your voice slide smoothly through all the letter-sounds.

Working your way together through the page,
read to your learner each blend, followed by the word:
  fl … flag,
then ask your learner to read it to you:
  fl … flag.

You can use a card, or your hand, to cover up
the words below the one you're concentrating on.

The next time through the page, you drop out of reading -
ask your learner to read each blend followed by the word.

Tick the correct blends and words.

If your learner struggles with a blend or a word,
wait four seconds and say it correctly, then underline it and
move on.

After your learner has tried all the words, coach
any underlined words.

Repeat this page at the start of your next session.

Coach read each blend and word, then ask your learner to read it to you.

Next, ask your learner to read them all out without prompting.

✓✓   ✓✓   ✓✓

fl	flag	gr	grin	sw	swim
sn	snot	tw	twit	bl	blend
sl	slip	tr	trick	pl	plan
br	brick	cr	crops	gl	glad
sp	spot	cl	clap	dr	drum
dw	dwell	scr	scrap	pr	pram
spl	split	str	strap	squ	squid
qu	quit	sk	skip	fr	frog
st	stand	thr	thrill	sm	smut

Coach

Blending practice

Ask your learner to read each word to you.

Use a card, or your hand, to cover up
the words below the one you're concentrating on.

Tick every correct word.

If your learner misreads a word, or hesitates, wait four seconds
then say the word correctly in a neutral voice. After your learner
has repeated the word correctly, underline it and move on.

After your learner has tried all the words, coach
any underlined words.

Repeat this page at the start of your next session.

Be patient! This could take several sessions.

slop

spat

spill

tram

sprig

sprog

brag

brush

drip

drop

plus

skull

skill

swim

swell

crab

cred

drab

drug

glad

Clap! Clap! That's good, ... !

Coach

Phew! Made it!

You and your learner have just made a huge breakthrough.
You now know that your learner will become a fluent reader.

reading practice

If all the words are right, tick the sentence.

If your learner misreads a word, or hesitates, wait four seconds
then say the word correctly in a neutral voice. After your learner
has repeated the word correctly, underline it and move on.

After your learner has tried all the sentences, coach
any underlined words.

When every sentence has been ticked twice, remember to
write in your learner's name.

Tip

When you have finished reading all the sentences on a page
or the Reading for Fun, encourage discussion with your learner.
This will further develop reading for meaning. Negative comments
from your learner such as 'that was boring' or 'that joke is so lame'
are just as valid and productive as any other observations.
This will show you that your learner is reading for meaning, and is
not merely 'barking at print'.

Learner read:

tick   tick

I trod in dog muck. It is on the clog.

Is the dog muck on the clog?

Yes the dog muck is on the clog.

The big fat cat trod on the frog.

The frog trod on the fat slug.

The fat slug sat on a bug.

The drab red crab sits in the sand.

Stop the tram and jump on.

I am glad the big blob ran off.

Sam and Pam drop the big bag.

I can swim and Bob and Dan and Fran can swim.

The cat spat at the dog.

The dog spat back at the cat.

Let us plod on to the pub.

Sam and I slip in the mud.

I quit.

Clap! Clap! That's good, ... !

Reading for Fun

Coach and learner have a go at these tongue twisters:

clap trap   clap trap   clap trap   clap trap

slap dash   slap dash   slap dash   slap dash

Coach

more **Blending** practice

Ask your learner to read each word to you.

Use a card or your hand to cover up the next word below.

Tick the correct words.

If your learner misreads a word, correct it, underline, and move on.

After your learner has tried all the words, coach
any underlined words.

When every word has been ticked twice,
write in your learner's name.

Learner read:

✓   ✓

glib

smug

club

clod

pram

press

flab

fret

frizz

snub

snog

twin

twit

grab

grub

bled

strap

strop

scum

scab

Clap! Clap! That's very good, ... !

Coach

reading practice

If all the words are right, tick the sentence.

If your learner misreads a word, correct it, underline, and move on.

After your learner has tried all the sentences, coach
any underlined words.

When every sentence has been ticked twice, remember to
write in your learner's name.

Tip

Focus on your learner's interests, and look at words about
fishing, football, celebrities, cooking, whatever. You will be
amazed. One of our learners could read BMW and Maserati
before we had even covered capital letters; another learner
could read Emmerdale and Coronation Street when we were
only a third of the way through this book.
Even the most reluctant reader will want to learn how to read
the names of family members and friends.

Fran the frog met Slob the slug.

That was the end of Slob the slug.

The dog sits in the cat flap and the cat sits in the pig pen.

The fish flaps and flips and flops in the sand on the land.

Mum has a big pram for the twins.

The fox grabs the hen and one of her chicks.

I hit the box with a big club.

The bug and the grub dug in the sand.

The twit has a smug grin. I will snub him.

The clod is a snob and I will snub him as well.

I quit.

Coach

Look Write Say

More everyday words that **don't follow easy rules**
and have to be learned by the *Look Write Say* method.

In the top line, point at any word and read it, then ask your learner
to read the word to you.
Don't read the letters separately - **say the whole word** - because
your learner is **MEMORISING the SHAPE of the WHOLE WORD.**

Make sure you cover each word at least twice.

Ask your learner to read you the words in the next section, unprompted.
Tick correct words, otherwise wait four seconds and say
the word correctly, then underline it.

Coach any underlined words.

If your learner still has difficulty with a word, write it on a piece

of spare paper, saying the word as you write.

Then ask your learner to copy your word, up to ten times,

saying the word as they are writing it.

This is a useful technique for any word

your learner struggles with, now or later.

Ask your learner to read each sentence to you, then either tick it
or correct any misread words and underline them.

After your learner has tried all the sentences, coach
any underlined words.

Repeat this page at the start of your next session.

Coach read each word, then learner read it:

now   two   she   go   goes   her

Learner read:

✓✓   ✓✓   ✓✓

she   her   two

go   goes   now

Learner read sentences:

tick   tick

Gran and Stan go to the shop now, to get

eggs and bran for a flan, and for flap jacks.

Fran goes to the shop as well, but

she gets her eggs from the two hens in her den.

She goes now and gets two big eggs for Dan.

Gran and Stan go to the pub with Fran and Dan.

Fran gets a rum and black.

Gran has a quick one - well two -

then she and Stan get up and go.

.... has two ticks. Well done!

Coach

ng

For the words at the top of the page, read each word to your learner and then ask your learner to read it to you.

Then ask your learner to read down the columns, unprompted, and tick every word read correctly without hesitation.

If your learner misreads a word, or hesitates, wait four seconds then say the word correctly in a neutral voice. After your learner has repeated the word correctly, underline it and move on.

After your learner has tried all the words, coach any underlined words.

Repeat this page at the start of your next session.

Coach read each word, then learner read it:

ring   sang   king   song   thing   bring   bang   long

Learner read down the columns:

✓✓   ✓✓

long	along
ding	bang
ding dong	bang bang
sing	ring
rang	rung
song	sang
twang	clang
bring	king
slang	pong
wing	gang
hang	hung
sting	stung
swing	sling
thing	zing

Coach

ng practice

Ask your learner to read the sentences.

If all the words are right, tick the sentence.

If your learner misreads a word, correct it, underline, and move on.

After your learner has tried all the sentences, coach
any underlined words.

When every sentence has been ticked twice, remember to
write in your learner's name.

Learner read:

tick   tick

Ding-dong, ding-dong, the bell rang and rang.

The gong rings: clang, clang, clang.

Swing the thing and it will ring.

Sing a song of six pigs. No, sing a song of ten hens.

Mad Max is in the gang and he has a gun.

Get him to sling the gun.

It is a big no to guns and gangs.

That long red thing is a fox.

The fox has big fangs.

Zac wed Jill, and now he has a ring on his finger.

Zac said Jill has one as well - a big ring on her finger.

.... **can read well now.**

tick   tick

Coach

Word Sums

Later on, your learner will discover how to divide long words
into syllables.

For now, you will plant a seed by doing word sums,
that is, adding two words together to make a third.

up + set = upset

Ask your learner to read the two words and then the third.

If your learner hesitates or faces a problem,
wait four seconds and correct in the usual, neutral way, then
underline the word.

After your learner has tried all the words, coach
any underlined words.

Repeat this page at the start of your next session.

When every line has been ticked twice, write in
your learner's name.

Learner read:

tick   tick

up + set	=	upset
cat + nap	=	catnap
rag + bag	=	ragbag
lap + top	=	laptop
ding + bat	=	dingbat
fox + trot	=	foxtrot
sing + song	=	singsong
swing + bin	=	swingbin
quick + step	=	quickstep
grand + ma	=	grandma
grand + pa	=	grandpa

.... **can read a lot.**

Coach

Look Write Say

More everyday words that **don't follow easy rules**
and have to be learned by the *Look Write Say* method.

In the top line, point at any word and read it, then ask your learner
to read the word to you.
Don't read the letters separately - **say the whole word** - because
your learner is **MEMORISING the SHAPE of the WHOLE WORD**.

Make sure you cover each word at least twice.

Ask your learner to read you the words in the next section, unprompted.
Tick correct words, otherwise wait four seconds and say
the word correctly, then underline it.

Coach any underlined words.

If your learner still has difficulty with a word, write it on a piece

of spare paper, saying the word as you write.

Then ask your learner to copy your word, up to ten times,

saying the word as they are writing it.

This is a useful technique for any word

your learner struggles with, now or later.

Ask your learner to read each sentence to you, then either tick it
or correct any misread words and underline them.

After your learner has tried all the sentences, coach
any underlined words.

Repeat this page at the start of your next session.

Coach point to a word and read it, then learner read it:

who   what   when   where   why   which

Learner read:

✓ ✓   ✓ ✓   ✓ ✓

who   where   when

what   which   why

Learner read the sentences:

tick   tick

The Big Flapjack Upset - what a ding-dong!

Who has got Fran and Grandma's box of flapjacks?

Where are the flapjacks?

Glen hid them in his den.

In his den? When?

Which one of us will go to his den and

get the flapjacks? Who will go?

Fran will go and get them. Why Fran?

The flapjacks are Fran and Grandma's.

Well well, what an upset!

What a lot .... can read!

Coach

reading practice

This reading exercise will revise all the skills your learner has
acquired so far.

Ask your learner to read each sentence.
If all the words are right, tick the sentence.
If your learner misreads a word, correct it, underline, and move on.

After your learner has tried all the sentences, coach
any underlined words.

Learner read:

tick   tick

My twin Fred has a laptop. I wish I had a laptop.

Fred is a rat-bag. He is not a rat-bag. Yes he is.

Glub. Fred is a ding-bat and he is a twit and a clot.

Now I am upset. I am upset for my pal Fred.

Who has had a catnap? The cat had a catnap

and the dog had a catnap.

Here is a smug man. He is a snob. What a smug snob!

Where is the red pram? The red pram is with Fred.

This club is for us. We can sing a song here.

Grab the big fat pig or he will run off.

Grandma and grandpa can do the fox-trot.

I am glad. I quit for now.

Now .... can read long words.

Coach

ai as in rain

In the top line, point to each word, read it, and ask your learner
to read the word to you.

Below, tick every correct word.
If your learner misreads a word, correct it, underline, and move on.

After your learner has tried all the words, coach
any underlined words.

If all the words are right, tick the sentence.
If your learner misreads a word, correct it, underline, and move on.

After your learner has tried all the sentences, coach
any underlined words.

Repeat this page at the start of your next session.

Coach read each word, then learner read it:

rain	pail	wait	drain	main	brain
hail	train	plain	Spain	gain	again

Learner read:

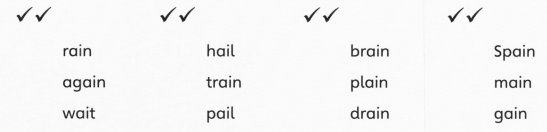

rain	hail	brain	Spain
again	train	plain	main
wait	pail	drain	gain

Learner read sentences:

tick   tick

The rain in Spain is on the plain.

Dick and Ali wait for a train in a hail storm in Spain.

Where is the train?

The train is not yet in Spain.

What a pain, said Dick.

Yes, it is a pain, said Quin.

We wait for a train in Spain in the rain, yet again.

Yes, in vain, that is plain!

I got a pain in my brain, so I quit, for now.

It is plain that .... is reading well, again.

Reading for Fun

Fun fact: The starfish has no brain.

Coach

Look Write Say

A few more everyday words that **don't follow easy rules**
and have to be learned by the *Look Write Say* method.

In the top line, point at any word and read it, then ask your learner
to read the word to you.
Don't read the letters separately - **say the whole word** - because
your learner is **MEMORISING the SHAPE of the WHOLE WORD**.

Make sure you cover each word at least twice.

Ask your learner to read you the words in the next section, unprompted.
Tick correct words, otherwise wait four seconds and say
the word correctly, then underline it.

Coach any underlined words.

If your learner still has difficulty with a word, write it on a piece

of spare paper, saying the word as you write.

Then ask your learner to copy your word, up to ten times,

saying the word as they are writing it.

This is a useful technique for any word

your learner struggles with, now or later.

Ask your learner to read each sentence to you, then either tick it
or correct any misread words and underline them.

After your learner has tried all the sentences, coach
any underlined words.

Repeat this page at the start of your next session.

Coach point to a word and read it, then learner read it:

so   do   there   me   how   you

Learner read:

do   there   how

me   so   you

Learner read the sentences:

tick   tick

The man from Spain said how do you do.

So where is the man from Spain who said how do you do?

There is the man from Spain who said how do you do.

So which one is the man from Spain?

That one there is the man from Spain.

So that one there is the man from Spain.

He said how do you do to me.

And he said how do you do to me.

And to me.

So which one is the man from Spain?

Not that again!

.... **is reading well again!**

Coach

ay as in day

In the top line, point to each word, read it, and ask your learner to read the word to you.

Below, tick every correct word.
If your learner misreads a word, or hesitates, wait four seconds then say the word correctly in a neutral voice. After your learner has repeated the word correctly, underline it and move on.

After your learner has tried all the words, coach any underlined words.

If all the words are right, tick the sentence.
If your learner misreads a word, correct it, underline, and move on.

After your learner has tried all the sentences, coach any underlined words.

Repeat this page at the start of your next session.

Your learner is now ready to read **King Rat and the Lab Rats** from our range of reading books which support *Yes we can read*.

Coach read each word, then learner read it:

pay	lay	may	jay	say	bay
way	hay	gay	ray	day	hay

Learner read:

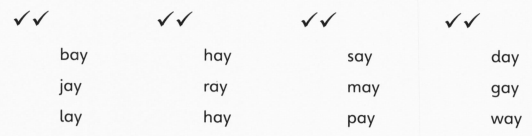

bay	hay	say	day
jay	ray	may	gay
lay	hay	pay	way

Learner read sentences:

tick   tick

I say, what a day! said Ray to Jay.

We will not stay in today, no way, said May.

I say let's go and play in the sun, said Fay.

Yes, let's get away and play today.

Then we can play in the hay! said Fay.

So, Ray, Jay, May and Fay

went off to the stacks of hay,

to play away the day, in the sun.

Yes, we can say .... is reading well today.

Reading for Fun

What do you do when two snails have a big tiff?

Let them slug it out.

Coach

ai and **ay** practice

If all the words are right, tick the sentence.
If your learner misreads a word, correct it, underline, and move on.

After your learner has tried all the sentences, coach
any underlined words.

Learner read:

tick   tick

Today Ray waits for the train, in the rain.

The train is not here yet, and he is wet.

Will he stay? The rain stops,

and here are May and Jay.

Now the train is here. Quick, get on!

Ray, May and Jay get on the train

and go away for the day.

We can say it again, ... is reading well.

tick   tick

Coach

Look Write Say

One more batch of words that **don't follow easy rules**
and have to be learned by the *Look Write Say* method.

In the top line, point at any word and read it, then ask your learner
to read the word to you.
Don't read the letters separately - **say the whole word** - because
your learner is **MEMORISING the SHAPE of the WHOLE WORD**.

Make sure you cover each word at least twice.

Ask your learner to read you the words in the next section, unprompted.
Tick correct words, otherwise wait four seconds and say
the word correctly, then underline it.

Coach any underlined words.

If your learner still has difficulty with a word, write it on a piece

of spare paper, saying the word as you write.

Then ask your learner to copy your word, up to ten times,

saying the word as they are writing it.

This is a useful technique for any word

your learner struggles with, now or later.

Ask your learner to read each sentence to you, then either tick it
or correct any misread words and underline them.

After your learner has tried all the sentences, coach
any underlined words.

Repeat this page at the start of your next session.

Coach point to a word and read it, then learner read it:

your   eye   says   girl   bird

Learner read:

✓ ✓   ✓ ✓   ✓ ✓

     says   your   eye

     girl   bird

Learner read the sentences:

tick   tick

The posh girl from Spain says, "How do you do?"

"I am well," I say, with one eye on the bird. It is a tit.

"What a day! What a day!" sings the bird in the sun.

"I felt a drop of rain in my eye," says the posh girl.

"A drop of rain in your eye?" I say.

"Yes, a drop of rain in my eye," the posh girl says.

"It is still hot," I say. "That is the main thing."

The girl says, "Do you sing? Let's sing with the bird."

We sing, "What a day! What a day!"

Well done .... , we say!

Coach

Vowels and their alphabet names

Tell your learner that vowels are the five special, super letters.
Turn to pages 14 and 15 and see if your learner can pick out the vowels.
If not, point out that **a, e, i, o** and **u** have coloured backgrounds.

Now your learner needs to know the alphabet names of the vowels.

Tell your learner their alphabet names are: **ay, ee, eye, oh, you.**

If your learner has difficulty remembering which letters are vowels,
they can see pages 14 and 15 for the five letters with coloured
backgrounds.

When your learner knows the new vowel names, explain that
the **letter-sounds** we already know are the **short** vowel sounds,
and the new **alphabet names** make the **long** vowel sounds.

Once your learner is easily pronouncing all the short and long vowels,
you can race each other, to see who is fastest down the list without a
mistake. Best of three?

Tip

Make up your own short song about **ay ee eye oh you** . . .
. . . if you both know the song "Old MacDonald had a Farm"
try singing it with the chorus changed to **ay ee eye oh you**!

Several of our adult learners surprised us with their knowledge of
vowels and consonants, even though they could not read at all
to start with . . .
. . . they were Countdown fans!

Coach and learner in turn, read the five as short vowels:

a   e   i   o   u

Both read these alphabet names as long vowels:

a   e   i   o   u

Learner read across:

✓ ✓ ✓ ✓   ✓ ✓ ✓ ✓

short a	long a
short e	long e
short i	long i
short o	long o
short u	long u

Learner read long and short vowels:

✓ ✓ ✓ ✓

short	a
long	e
short	u
short	i
long	a
long	o
short	e
long	u
long	i
short	o

Well done .... , we say!

Coach

silent e

Tell your learner that when it's at the end of a word,
the letter -**e** has a magic power. . .

that -**e** at the end of the word usually does **two** things:
it tells you the sound of the previous vowel is a **long** vowel sound
and the final -**e** is **silent**.

For example,
    you read **rat** with a **short a**,
        and you read **rate** with a **long a**, and
            you don't pronounce the **e** at the end - it is a **silent e**.

In the first part, point to each word, read it, and ask your learner
to read the word to you.

Below, tick, or correct and underline as usual.

After your learner has tried all the words, coach
any underlined words.

Repeat this page at the start of your next session.

Coach read:

When you see **-e** at the end of a word, the previous vowel is **long**.

Coach read each word, then learner read it:

pin	pine	hop	hope
pan	pane	lob	lobe
hid	hide	tub	tube
fad	fade	fat	fate
rid	ride	kit	kite

Learner only:

✓   ✓   ✓   ✓

note	mate
hope	mute
hate	cute
cope	cane
cube	bite
Kate	ride
stride	Dave
crave	brave

Coach

silent e practice

This exercise requires your learner to recognise
words with and without the **silent e**.

Before you start, point out that the **silent e** rule still applies if
there is a **s** at the very end, after the **e**. . . for example, **rates**.

Tick, or correct and underline as usual.

After your learner has tried all the word pairs, coach
any underlined words.

Repeat this page at the start of your next session.

Learner read down the columns:

✓✓   ✓✓   ✓✓

fad	fade	tub	tube	hates
mad	made	dud	dude	likes
cam	came	cut	cute	makes
Sam	same	cub	cube	takes
dam	dame	hid	hide	smiles
can	cane	rid	ride	hides
Dan	Dane	Sid	side	gales
Jan	Jane	kit	kite	fines
cap	cape	spit	spite	lines
gap	gape	quit	quite	cubes
tap	tape	dim	dime	tubes
fat	fate	Tim	time	gropes
mat	mate	prim	prime	grapes
rat	rate	fin	fine	braves
cod	code	win	wine	stripes
mod	mode	pin	pine	hopes
rod	rode	spin	spine	
Dom	dome	pip	pipe	
Tom	tome	grip	gripe	
pop	pope	trip	tripe	
cop	cope	strip	stripe	
pet	Pete			

.... has made a big jump!

89

Coach

silent e more practice

Here your learner will practise
words with the **silent e**, with and without a **s**.

If all the words are right, tick the sentence.
If your learner misreads a word, correct it, underline, and move on.

After your learner has tried all the sentences, coach
any underlined words.

Tip

Find out which songs or jingles your learner knows.
Type or write out the words of the song, and read and sing
the words together. Singing is a magical aid to learning and
making connections. One of our learners read the word 'Coke'
on a bottle and said, "Here's a song for you, Coach:
I'd like to teach the world to read."

Learner read the sentences:

Mike has a black hat. His wife Jane made it for him.

When she gave it to him he said, "I like that, thank you!"

But he hates his black hat and he hopes it gets lost.

Mike has a mate, Dave, and Dave likes the hat.

Dave says, "I like your black hat, Mike.

May I take it, just for a bit?"

Dave says, with a smile, "I will bring it back!"

Mike says, "Yes, that's fine."

Mike smiles as well. "Go on Dave, take it!"

Jane says, "Where's your hat?"

"Dave has it," says Mike. "He likes it, and he will

take it for a ride on his bike."

"But I made it for you! How long will he take it for?"

"Just for a bit!"

.... **has made a big jump with**
                                    the silent e at the end of words.

Reading for Fun

What do you call a vampire that can lift up cars?

Jack u la.

What bird can lift the most?

A crane.

Coach

oo

double o makes the **oo** sound which can be short, or can be longer:

the shorter **oo** . . . look, cook, book,   and
the longer **oo** . . . moo, cool, school.

You will find that your learner will cope with the difference naturally,
and will not need to be taught the two groups separately.

At the top of the page, read each word to your learner,
then ask your learner to read it to you.

Then move to the list
to see what your learner can read without prompting.

As usual tick the words your learner knows.
If your learner misreads a word, correct it, underline, and move on.

After your learner has tried all the words, coach
any underlined words.

Repeat this page at the start of your next session.

Coach read each word, then learner read it:

too   moon   soon   book   cook   look   foot

Learner read:

✓   ✓

foot

cool

loot

book

hoot

soon

boots

fool

food

moo

croon

wood

shoot

good

Coach

oo practice

If all the words are right, tick the sentence.

If your learner misreads a word, or hesitates, wait four seconds then say the word correctly in a neutral voice. After your learner has repeated the word correctly, underline it and move on.

After your learner has tried all the sentences, coach any underlined words.

Tip

Remember, you can always go back to revise an earlier page if your learner has forgotten particular letter-sounds or words. (The contents are listed at the front of the book.)

Learner read:

✓   ✓

Dog poo has to go in the dog poo bin.

Yes, we will take the dog poo to the dog poo bin.

Lob it in!

They will shoot the fox if he stays in the woods.

I will look in the cook book for food that is good to cook.

They tell me **Yes we can read** is a good book.

Soon my mates and I will swim in the pool in the woods.

I put my boots in the boot box.

It is too soon for the moon to rise.

It is too hot to go on the Tube, so I will go on foot.

I quit for today.

...................................'s reading is good!

Reading for Fun

Coach and learner have a go at this tongue twister:
Moose noshing much mush, moose noshing much mush.

Give me food and I live.

Give me a drink and I die.

What am I?

Fire.

Coach

ee

double e makes the **ee** sound, like a mouse squeaking.

In the top line, point to each word, read it, and ask your learner
to read the word to you.

Below, give every correct word a tick.
If your learner misreads a word, correct it, underline, and move on.

After your learner has tried all the words, coach
any underlined words.

Repeat this page at the start of your next session.

Coach read each word, then learner read it:

see   tree   need   three   sleep   keep   green

Learner read:

✓   ✓

green

feel

keep

need

tree

three

feet

sleep

sheep

street

bees

cheek

free

been

Coach

ee practice

If all the words are right, tick the sentence.

If your learner misreads a word, correct it, underline, and move on.

After your learner has tried all the sentences, coach
any underlined words.

Learner read:

The bees feel free to go to sleep in the hive.

Why do the bees feel free to go to sleep there?

The queen bee is back in the hive, so the bees can sleep.

The queen bee has been in the green trees.

Three of the bees are still in the green trees in your street.

Those three bees will soon be back now the queen is home.

Then those three bees can go to sleep too.

I will quit soon.

.....................................'s reading is good. Keep it up!

Reading for Fun

What do you call a deer that has no eyes?
No eye deer (no idea).

Coach and learner have a go at this tongue twister:
Greek grapes Greek grapes Greek grapes Greek grapes

Coach

oo and **ee** practice

If all the words are right, tick the sentence.

If your learner misreads a word, correct it, underline, and move on.

After your learner has tried all the sentences, coach
any underlined words.

A Trip to Green Wood Farm to See the Sheep

Put your foot in this green boot to see if it fits.

These green boots are too big for my feet.

Well, put on the black boots then. You can see if they fit.

Fine, the black boots seem okay on my poor old feet.

It seems to me they look good too.

Now we can go to Green Wood Farm and see the sheep.

In those boots you can step in the mud.

Yes, last time we went to Green Wood Farm I stood in

the slop and the poo, but I did not have these good boots.

Keep the boots on, and then we can see the sheep,

and feed the geese and the three ducks.

Good! Three cheers for ....

Reading for Fun

Fun fact:	Queen bees only sting other queen bees.

Coach

oi

In the top line, point to each word, read it, and ask your learner
to read the word to you.

Below, give every correct word a tick.
If your learner misreads a word, correct it, underline, and move on.

After your learner has tried all the words, coach
any underlined words.

Repeat this page at the start of your next session.

Coach read each word, then learner read it:

oil   boil   soil   coin   coil   join

Learner read:

✓   ✓

join

oil

boils

coil

Moira

toil

soil

broil

foil

spoil

coins

quoits

void

avoid

joint

Coach

oi practice

If all the words are right, tick the sentence.

If your learner misreads a word, or hesitates, wait four seconds then say the word correctly in a neutral voice. After your learner has repeated the word correctly, underline it and move on.

After your learner has tried all the sentences, coach any underlined words.

Omid and I dug in the soil and there was an old coin.

Moira had a red boil on her leg and she got snake oil for it.

Snake oil on a boil? Yes, snake oil on her boil.

Let's play quoits. What is quoits?

A quoit is a ring made of thick rope,

and you chuck it on a big stick.

What is the point? The point is to win points.

You win a point when you get the quoit on the stick.

I like loin chops, and so I will cook this loin chop in oil.

Will you have a boiled sweet? No thank you,

boiled sweets spoil my teeth, so I avoid boiled sweets.

Top points! .... **can read well.**

Coach

oy

In the top line, point to each word, read it, and ask your learner
to read the word to you.

Below, give every correct word a tick.
If your learner misreads a word, correct it, underline, and move on.

After your learner has tried all the words, coach
any underlined words.

Repeat this page at the start of your next session.

Coach read each word, then learner read it:

boy   toy   Roy   coy   annoy   joy

Learner read:

✓ ✓

joy

boy

toy

toys

Roy

Troy

coy

cloy

annoy

ahoy

boys

soya

Coach

oy practice

If all the words are right, tick the sentence.

If your learner misreads a word, correct it, underline, and move on.

After your learner has tried all the sentences, coach
any underlined words.

Tip

Send your learner a letter or post card. Use the words you have
covered and, if possible, use a special word you have learned
through *Look Write Say*. It will be a real thrill for your learner,
showing that they can read without you there, and it will further
develop reading for meaning.

One of our older learners, who was convinced she would
never be able to read without her coach there, greeted him
with the letter in her hand, beaming, "I can read! Yes I can!"

This boy can join the club.

What is the boy's name?

This boy's name is Troy.

Can he bring his toys with him?

Yes, that boy Troy can bring all his toys.

And Troy can bring his mate Roy too.

But Roy is not a good boy.

Roy took Joy's best toy, and broke it.

Roy spoils the fun at the club.

Will you tell Troy not to bring his mate Roy?

No, I will tell Roy's mum he annoys us,

and he spoils the fun for the rest of us.

Then she will not bring her boy Roy to the club.

What joy! .... can read well.

Coach

-y

-y (at the end of a word) is usually pronounced as **short i**.
For example, after a double consonant, like **happy**
and many names end with **-y**, like **Bobby**.

In the top line, point to each word, read it, and ask your learner
to read the word to you.

Below, tick every correct word.
If your learner misreads a word, correct it, underline, and move on.

After your learner has tried all the words, coach
any underlined words.

Repeat this page at the start of your next session.

Coach read each word, then learner read it:

Bobby   piggy   silly   merry   Betty   happy

Learner read:

✓ ✓

happy

Bobby

penny

Willy

merry

jolly

Noddy

berry

messy

jazzy

silly

hippy

jiffy

Betty

fuzzy

Twiggy

bossy

Coach

-y practice

If all the words are right, tick the sentence.

If your learner misreads a word, correct it, underline, and move on.

After your learner has tried all the sentences, coach
any underlined words.

Tip

Focus on your learner's interests, and look at words about
fishing, football, celebrities, cooking, whatever.
You will be amazed.
Even the most reluctant reader will want to learn how to read
the names of family members and friends.

Learner read:

Polly and Meera live in a big messy flat with

Bobby the happy puppy.

Bobby is happy but he can be silly and greedy.

So from time to time the girls have to be bossy

with Bobby the silly puppy.

When he sees a bird he runs to get it. How silly is that?

Bobby ate six cakes and then he had a funny tummy.

How silly and greedy is that?

One day he had a fizzy drink and went dizzy.

Polly and Meera had to take Bobby the puppy

to the vet in a big hurry.

The vet said, "Bobby will live, but he is such a silly puppy."

.... **is jolly good at reading now.**

Reading for Fun

Why has Noddy got a hat with a bell on it?
Noddy has a hat with a bell on it 'cos he is a plonker.

Coach and learner have a go at this tongue twister:
Peggy Babcock   Peggy Babcock   Peggy Babcock

Coach

-ing add-ons (suffixes)

This will prepare your learner, in a non-threatening way,
for reading longer words.

At the top of the page, read each pair of words to your learner,
then ask your learner to read that pair to you.

Then ask your learner to read the pairs of words down each column.
Tick every pair of words your learner reads correctly first go.

If your learner misreads a word, or hesitates, wait four seconds
then say the word pair correctly in a neutral voice. After your
learner has repeated the word pair correctly, underline it and
move on.

After your learner has tried all the word pairs, coach
any underlined words.

Repeat this page at the start of your next session.

Coach read each word, then learner read it:

see seeing   sing singing   ring ringing   shop shopping

chop chopping   rob robbing   cook cooking

Learner read down the columns:

✓ ✓   ✓ ✓

see	seeing		swim	swimming
fit	fitting		look	looking
sit	sitting		sniff	sniffing
chop	chopping		sin	sinning
rob	robbing		hug	hugging
chat	chatting		bug	bugging
cook	cooking		skip	skipping
sing	singing		bat	batting
pin	pinning		chat	chatting
win	winning		send	sending
faint	fainting		lend	lending

Coach

ing practice

If all the words are right, tick the sentence.
If your learner misreads a word, correct it, underline, and move on.

After your learner has tried all the sentences, coach
any underlined words.

Learner read:

 ✓ ✓

Pops the dog is running at the dog track today.

We are pinning our hopes on Pops the dog winning.

Pops is sniffing smells and he is looking good.

We must stop chatting as the dogs are off and

Pops is running now.

Pops is running like the wind, and we are singing

Pops is the tops. Go! Go! Go, Pops!

Now Pops is winning, and we are jumping and skipping,

and running to get our winnings.

A man is hugging Pops, and he is still looking fit.

Now we are singing Pops is the tops, Pops is the best!

.... **is reading well today.**

Coach

-er and **-est** add-ons

At the top of the page, read each word along the line to your learner, then ask your learner to read it to you.

Then ask your learner to read each word pair down the columns.
Tick each word pair your learner reads correctly first go.
If your learner misreads a word, correct it, underline, and move on.

After your learner has tried all the word pairs, coach any underlined words.

Repeat this page at the start of your next session.

Coach read each word, then learner read it:

bigger	fatter	hotter	redder	colder	longer
greenest	longest	fattest	quickest	hottest	dullest

Learner read down the columns:

✓✓   ✓✓

big	bigger		green	greenest
fat	fatter		long	longest
hot	hotter		fat	fattest
red	redder		quick	quickest
long	longer		hot	hottest
cold	colder		dull	dullest
quick	quicker		lush	lushest
old	older		plush	plushest
green	greener		big	biggest
plush	plusher		old	oldest

Coach

-er and **-est** practice

Ask your learner to read each sentence.
If all the words are right, tick the sentence.
If your learner misreads a word, correct it, underline, and move on.

After your learner has tried all the sentences, coach
any underlined words.

Your learner is now ready to read **Sandy the Snake Saves the Day**
from our range of reading books which support *Yes we can read*.

Learner read:

✓   ✓

That pig is looking fatter.

Fatter? It is the fattest pig in Green Wood Farm.

Our best runner is getting quicker.

Quicker? She is the quickest runner we have.

Is my face looking redder?

Redder? It is the reddest face I have ever seen.

Is the tree getting greener?

Greener? It is the greenest tree in the woods.

Am I older than you?

Older? You are the oldest boy here.

It is much hotter today.

Hotter? Today is the hottest day ever.

The girl is getting bigger now.

Bigger? Yes she is much bigger.

My nose is getting longer.

Longer? It is not the longest nose I have ever seen.

We hope this was not the dullest and longest page ever.

.... is getting much quicker at reading.

Reading for Fun

What do you get if you cross a duck with a fire-work?
A fire-quacker.
If you are in a hole, it is better to stop digging.
Fun fact: The eye of an ostrich is bigger than its brain.

Coach

-ed add-ons

Explain that **-ed** at the end of words is usually pronounced
with the softest letter-sound **d**, as in **look**(e)**d**.

At the top of the page read each pair of words to your learner, and
ask your learner to read it to you.
Then move along the line to the next pair.

Then ask your learner to read the pairs of words down the columns,
and tick every pair of words your learner reads correctly first go.

If your learner misreads a word, or hesitates, wait four seconds
then say the word pair correctly in a neutral voice. After your
learner has repeated the word pair correctly, underline it
and move on.

After your learner has tried all the word pairs, coach
any underlined words.

Repeat this page at the start of your next session.

Coach read each word, then learner read it:

hug hugged   tug tugged   look looked   cook cooked

shop shopped   chop chopped   skip skipped   clap clapped

Learner read down the columns:

✓✓   ✓✓

look	looked		book	booked
hug	hugged		trick	tricked
shop	shopped		lick	licked
chop	chopped		zip	zipped
spell	spelled		tug	tugged
clap	clapped		brag	bragged
drop	dropped		rain	rained
pin	pinned		train	trained
sin	sinned		spoon	spooned
sniff	sniffed		cook	cooked
bug	bugged		rob	robbed
drag	dragged		skip	skipped
prick	pricked		jump	jumped

Coach

-ed practice

If all the words are right, tick the sentence.

If your learner misreads a word, correct it, underline, and move on.

After your learner has tried all the sentences, coach
any underlined words.

Learner read:

The dog sniffed and sniffed, and then

the dog licked my nose.

I shopped and shopped until I dropped.

The man hugged and hugged the tree and then

he chopped it and felled it.

It rained and rained and then it stopped.

I pricked my hand on a rose thorn, and then

I pricked my hand again.

The con man tricked us and then he tricked us again.

So he had robbed us.

The girl skipped and skipped and then she jumped.

I looked and looked for the puppy and then

the puppy rushed back home.

It is time we clapped ....

Reading for Fun

A boy stepped off the bus and asked the man with a dog,
"Does your dog bite?"
"No," said the man, "my dog does not bite."
The boy stroked the dog. Then the dog nipped the boy.
"You said your dog does not bite," said the boy.
The man grinned and said, "That dog is not my dog!"

Coach

-ing **-er** **-est** **-ed** practice

If all the words are right, tick the paragraph.

If your learner misreads a word, correct it, underline, and move on.

After your learner has tried all the paragraphs, coach
any underlined words.

When the biggest robber robbed the shop, I looked

shocked and he rushed off.

Billy is the fattest cook. He cooked some chops.

When Billy was flipping pancakes, he kept dropping

the pancakes on the floor.

There are two ducklings. One is smaller, the other is bigger.

The bigger duckling has been swimming and swimming in

the greenest pond. It looked sweet.

Harry is a quick runner, but Jenny can run a bit quicker.

Then when Jenny got fed up and stopped, she lost the race.

It was a rainy day and the boys got wetter and wetter,

but that did not stop the biggest boy from singing in the rain.

Who was skipping and who was hopping along the street?

The girl skipped, and a bird hopped, along the street.

Have you finished? Yes, I have finished for today.

.... **can read much longer words.**

Coach

ea

The letter blend **ea** usually makes one of these two vowel sounds:
either the long **e** sound, like **meat**, **bead**
or the short **e** sound, like **head**, **bread**.
(There are exceptions, and they will require the *Look Write Say* approach.)

First your learner will practise **ea** as in **tea**.

At the top of the page, read each word to your learner,
then ask your learner to read it to you.

Below, tick every word read correctly.
If your learner misreads a word, correct it, underline, and move on.

After your learner has tried all the words, coach
any underlined words.

Tick each sentence if all the words are right.
If your learner misreads a word, correct it, underline, and move on.

After your learner has tried all the sentences, coach
any underlined words.

Repeat this page at the start of your next session.

Coach read each word, then learner read it:

read	tea	sea	team	each	meat
meal	dream	please	easy	teacher	leave

Learner read:

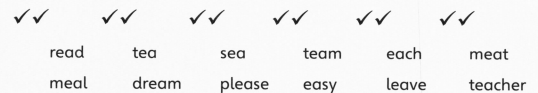

read	tea	sea	team	each	meat
meal	dream	please	easy	leave	teacher

Learner read:

I dream that I can swim in the sea.

In the sea?

Yes I dream I can swim in the sea.

Did that team beat the top team?

Yes that team beat the top team.

Make me a cup of tea please.

Yes I will make a cup of tea.

I will make two cups of tea, one for each of us.

I will read as I eat my meal.

Will he read the book as he eats his meal?

Yes he will read his book as he eats the meal.

Reading this was not easy.

The teacher said I can read well now.

.... **can read well.**

Reading for Fun

The more you take us, the more you leave us behind.
What are we?
Footsteps.

Coach

ea

Now your learner will practise **ea** as in **head**.

At the top of the page, read each word to your learner,
then ask your learner to read it to you.

Below, tick every word read correctly.
If your learner misreads a word, correct it, underline, and move on.

After your learner has tried all the words, coach
any underlined words.

Tick each sentence if all the words are right.
If your learner misreads a word, correct it, underline, and move on.

After your learner has tried all the sentences, coach
any underlined words.

Repeat this page at the start of your next session.

Coach read each word, then learner read it:

head	bread	ready	healthy	deaf
dead	heavy	dread	weather	spread

Learner read:

head	bread	ready	healthy	deaf
dead	heavy	dread	weather	spread

Learner read:

Spread butter and jam on your bread.

Yes I will spread butter and jam on my bread.

The snake bit the cat. I feel dread that the cat is dead.

Yes I am afraid the cat is dead.

It is raining and the weather is bad.

The weather has been bad for a long time.

Then I will take a hat if the weather is still bad.

I will take a hat to keep my head dry.

If we get rain hats we will be ready to go.

Hang on, I am not quite ready to go yet.

This box is heavy. It is very heavy.

Give me a hand with this heavy box.

.... **has read well today.**

Reading for Fun

Coach and learner have a go at these tongue twisters:

Cheap ship trip, cheap ship trip, cheap ship trip.

Fred fed Ted bread and Ted fed Fred bread.

Fun fact: Dust is made from dead skin.

Coach

ea practice

Tick each sentence if all the words are right.

If your learner misreads a word, or hesitates, wait four seconds then say the word correctly in a neutral voice. After your learner has repeated the word correctly, underline it and move on.

After your learner has tried all the sentences, coach any underlined words.

I have a bad cold in my head, so I will go to bed and hope

that the bad cold in my head gets better.

This case is hard to lift. It is very heavy.

No it is not very heavy, I mean I don't find it very heavy.

My boots and my belt are made of leather. Leather is

good for boots in wet weather.

I will have cheese and meat for my meal. I will put the

cheese and meat on bread, and then I will eat my meal.

In my dreams I swim in the sea.

You swim in the sea in your dreams? Like a fish?

Yes, I swim in the sea in my dreams.

What nice dreams!

Each time you read, your reading gets better.

Yes, your reading gets better each time you read.

.... **can read better.**

Coach

more **add-ons**

Some common add-ons are

-ful   -ly   -less   -ment   -ness   -some

At the top of the page, read to your learner each set
- word, add-on and longer word -
then ask your learner to read each set to you.

Then move to the word pairs,
to see how many your learner can read without any prompting.

Tick every pair your learner reads correctly first go.
If your learner misreads a word, correct it, underline, and move on.

After your learner has tried all the word pairs, coach
any underlined words.

Repeat this page at the start of your next session.

Coach read each word, then learner read it:

fear	-ful	fearful	love	-ly	lovely
care	-less	careless	pave	-ment	pavement
hand	-some	handsome	late	-ness	lateness

Learner read down the columns:

✓✓   ✓✓

late	lateness		safe	safely
hope	hopeful		pave	pavement
kind	kindness		tire	tiresome
hate	hateful		like	likely
age	ageless		dark	darkness
wise	wisely		wit	witless
enjoy	enjoyment		fear	fearsome
cool	coolness		spoon	spoonful
care	careless		mind	mindless
treat	treatment		joy	joyful
beast	beastly		ship	shipment

Coach

add-ons practice

Tick each sentence if all the words are right.

If your learner misreads a word, say it correctly, underline it, and move on.

After your learner has tried all the sentences, coach any underlined words.

Tip

> Remember, you can always go back to revise an earlier page
> if your learner has forgotten particular letter-sounds or words.
> (The contents are listed at the front of the book.)

Learner read:

✓   ✓

The names of the seven dwarfs are Doc, Happy, Grumpy,

Dopey, Sleepy, Sneezy and Bashful.

Bashful crossed the street safely and

shyly said, "Hello!" to Grumpy who was in a bad mood.

Doc wisely stayed away from Grumpy.

Happy skipped up hopefully, but there was

a coolness from Grumpy.

"Don't be so hateful," said Happy fearlessly.

"What Grumpy needs is some kindness," said Sleepy

waking up.

"Shall I give him a kiss?" asked Dopey.

"Not likely," said Grumpy.

Sneezy sneezed a big sneeze.

"Bless you!" said Happy.

.... **has made lovely progress.**

Reading for Fun

What kind of animals use nutcrackers?

Toothless squirrels

What do you give a sick bird?

Tweetment

Which bird is always short of breath?

A puffin

Coach

ew

Tell your learner **ew** is pronounced **you**.

At the top of the page, read each word to your learner,
then ask your learner to read it to you.

Below, tick every word read correctly.
If your learner misreads a word, correct it, underline, and move on.

After your learner has tried all the words, coach
any underlined words.

Tick each sentence if all the words are right.
If your learner misreads a word, correct it, underline, and move on.

After your learner has tried all the sentences, coach
any underlined words.

Repeat this page at the start of your next session.

Coach read each word, then learner read it:

chew	dew	drew	new	few	screw
blew	mew	crew	dew	pew	
strewn	flew	grew	Jew	stew	

Learner read:

few	dew	Jew	jewel
stew	blew	crew	chew
drew	flew	new	knew
mew	grew	screw	strewn

Learner read:

A new boy in our crew told me a new joke:

"What is green and red? . . . A frog in a food blender!"

That's not a new joke. It is as old as the hills.

I hate that joke. It makes me feel sick. It is not new

and it is not funny. When I think of that poor frog

strewn all over the blender I feel so sick.

Tell the new boy in your crew to stop telling bad jokes.

It is time he grew up. It is time you grew up too.

.... **can do lots of new things.**

Reading for Fun

I know a word of letters three.
Add two, and fewer will there be.
What is the word?
Few.

Coach

ue

Tell your learner **ue** (just like **ew**) is pronounced **you**.

At the top of the page, read each word to your learner,
then ask your learner to read it to you.

Below, tick every word read correctly.
If your learner misreads a word, correct it, underline, and move on.

After your learner has tried all the words, coach
any underlined words.

Tick each sentence if all the words are right.
If your learner misreads a word, correct it, underline, and move on.

After your learner has tried all the sentences, coach
any underlined words.

Repeat this page at the start of your next session.

Coach read each word, then learner read it:

clue	cue	glue	issue	blue	Sue
due	sue	argue	flue	true	gruesome

Learner read:

due	clue	glue	blue
Sue	sue	issue	argue
cue	flue	true	gruesome

Learner read:

Are you still feeling blue, Sue? Yes, it's true, I still feel blue.

It was that sick joke. That gruesome one set me off,

the joke about the frog in a blender.

Well I won't argue with you, Sue,

but I have not got a clue which joke you mean.

What do you mean, you have not got a clue?

The issue is the gruesome joke about a frog in a blender.

It is true, ... can read well now.

Reading for Fun

Coach and learner have a go at this tongue twister:
The blue bluebird blinks, the blue bluebird blinks.

What do you call the saddest bird in the world?
The blue tit.

Coach

ew and **ue** practice

Tick each paragraph if all the words are right.

If your learner misreads a word, or hesitates, wait four seconds then say the word correctly in a neutral voice. After your learner has repeated the word correctly, underline it and move on.

After your learner has tried all the text, coach any underlined words.

Learner read:

✓ ✓

I love your new blue jeans. Where did you get your new blue jeans? These blue jeans are not new, but I got them from the shopping mall. There are a few left in your size.

The crew on the jet plane flew to New York. When is the plane due in New York? It is due to arrive in New York at noon, New York time.

Who threw the chewing gum at the teacher?
Not me. I have no clue who threw the chewing gum.
Yes, it was you who threw the chewing gum.

Is it true that you grew two inches in a year?
Yes it is true that I grew two inches. I am now five foot and six inches tall. So, what is that in metres?

I don't like this stew. It sticks to the plate like glue.
I agree. The stew sticks like glue. Who cooked this stew?
Billy cooked the stew that sticks like glue.

It's true, ... can read very well.

Reading for Fun

Question:	Which three days begin with a T?
Answer:	Tuesday, Thursday and Today.

Coach

soft g

The letter-sound **g** can go soft on us.
Tell your learner that while the letter-sound **g** is called a hard **g**,
the same letter **g** can also have a soft sound, like the letter-sound **j**.

g is spoken soft, like the letter **j**, when it is followed by **e i** or **y**.

(Use *Look Write Say* for the exceptions, like **get, girl, give**.)

At the top of the page, read each word to your learner,
then ask your learner to read it to you.

Below, tick every word read correctly.
If your learner misreads a word, correct it, underline, and move on.

After your learner has tried all the words, coach
any underlined words.

Repeat this page at the start of your next session.

Coach read each word, then learner read it:

gentle   ginger   gym   stranger   danger   engine

age   cage   suggest   damage   gent   cabbage

Learner read:

✓ ✓   ✓ ✓   ✓ ✓   ✓ ✓

gent	German	ranger	magic
wage	page	Gemma	ginger
agent	danger	fringe	large
giant	gym	angel	Egypt
age	rage	baggage	gem
suggest	binge	sponge	range
huge	revenge	cage	change
stranger	bulge	George	gentle

Coach

soft g practice

Tick each sentence if all the words are right.

If your learner misreads a word, say it correctly, underline it, and move on.

After your learner has tried all the text, coach any underlined words.

Learner read:

✓   ✓

The Story of George the Jolly Green Giant

Is that George the jolly orange giant?

George the jolly orange giant?

No, he has changed into George the gentle green giant.

George the gentle green giant?

No, he has changed into George the magic green giant.

George the magic green giant?

No, he has changed into George the huge strange giant.

George the huge strange giant?

No, he has changed into Roger the German giant.

Roger the German giant?

No, he has changed back into George the jolly green giant.

George the jolly green giant likes huge ginger nuts.

No, George the jolly green giant likes huge orange Jaffa

cakes.

Magic, ... !

Reading for Fun

Fun fact:	King George the First of England did not speak English. He was born and raised in Germany.

Coach

igh

igh is pronounced as **long i**.
Tell your learner that here **gh** is silent. . . and tell them
after the silent **gh** there is usually a **t** which *is* pronounced.

At the top of the page, read each word to your learner,
then ask your learner to read it to you.

Below, tick every word read correctly.
If your learner misreads a word, correct it, underline, and move on.

After your learner has tried all the words, coach
any underlined words.

Tick each sentence if all the words are right.
If your learner misreads a word, correct it, underline, and move on.

After your learner has tried all the sentences, coach
any underlined words.

Repeat this page at the start of your next session.

Coach read each word, then learner read it:

high   sigh   sight   light   fight   right

Learner read:

right	sigh	light	night
high	sight	tight	bright
fight	fright	flight	might

Learner read:

Fight with all your might for

the right to light up the sky at night!

A man was driving a black truck.

His lights were not on.

A woman was crossing the street.

How did the man see the woman?

It was a light, bright sunny day.

I think we have got those tight fight words right now.

You are right! We can now read words like

high, sight and fright. Alright!

Right on! .... **got those all right.**

Reading for Fun

Coach and learner have a go at this tongue twister:
You've no need to light a night light
on a light night like tonight,
for a night light light's a slight light
and tonight's a night that's light.

Coach

-y

-y (at the end of a word) can be pronounced as **long i**.

At the top of the page, read each word to your learner,
then ask your learner to read it to you.

Below, tick every word read correctly.
If your learner misreads a word, correct it, underline, and move on.

After your learner has tried all the words, coach
any underlined words.

Tick each sentence if all the words are right.
If your learner misreads a word, correct it, underline, and move on.

After your learner has tried all the sentences, coach
any underlined words.

Repeat this page at the start of your next session.

Coach read each word, then learner read it:

by   cry   why   rely   deny   fly

Learner read:

fly	why	sky	dry
rely	my	fry	cry
July	try	shy	reply
spy	deny	pig-sty	

Learner read:

There is a fly buzzing by the pig's nose in the pig-sty.

Well it is July - you will get a fly in the pig-sty

from time to time on a dry day in July.

We can't rely on the pig to get rid of the fly,

let's get some fly-spray. I don't like to use fly-spray,

I will thwack the fly with this stick, that will kill the fly.

Be careful! I hope you don't hit the pig.

Oo! Is that a bat? No, it's just a bigger fly.

A bat is a fly-by-night.

You don't get bats on a dry bright day in July.

You can't deny .... reads well.

Reading for Fun

> Georgie Porgie pudding and pie
> kissed the girls and made them cry.
> Why?

Coach

-ied and **-ies**

-ied and **-ies** (at the ends of words) are pronounced with a **long i**.

At the top of the page, read each word to your learner,
then ask your learner to read it to you.

Below, tick every word read correctly.
If your learner misreads a word, or hesitates, wait four seconds
then say the word correctly in a neutral voice. After your learner
has repeated the word correctly, underline it and move on.

After your learner has tried all the words, coach
any underlined words.

Tick each sentence if all the words are right.
If your learner misreads a word, correct it, underline, and move on.

After your learner has tried all the sentences, coach
any underlined words.

Repeat this page at the start of your next session.

Coach read each word, then learner read it:

tried   fried   spies   denied   skies   replied

Learner read:

✓ ✓   ✓ ✓

dry	dried	dries	fry	fries	fried
try	tries	tried	cry	cried	cries
deny	denied	denies	rely	relied	relies
apply	applied	applies	defy	defies	defied
			reply	replies	replied

Learner read:

✓   ✓

I met my mate Ali in the park, where he works.

"On Monday it tried to rain," he said, "but there were only

a few drops. Today the skies are dry. I rely on rain, so

I will have to turn on the hose."

I said that I had applied for a job in the park, but that

so far they had not replied.

Ali said, "If they have not replied you can try again. I tried again,

and that time they replied and I got the job, as you can see!"

"Tyson tried for a job in the park, and he cried when

he failed to get the job," I said.

"Tyson cries all the time," Ali replied. "He is a wimp.

It can't be denied that Tyson cries a lot."

.... **has tried hard, and done well.**

Coach

soft c

The letter-sound **c** can go soft on us too (like **g** can).

Tell your learner that while the letter-sound **c** is called a hard **c**, the letter **c** can also have a soft sound, like the letter-sound **s**.

c is soft, like the letter-sound **s**, when followed by **e** or **i** or **y**.

At the top of the page, read each word to your learner, then ask your learner to read it to you.

Below, tick every word read correctly.
If your learner misreads a word, correct it, underline, and move on.

After your learner has tried all the words, coach any underlined words.

Repeat this page at the start of your next session.

Coach read each word, then learner read it:

cement   city   centre   cycle   Cilla

parcel   December   pencil   concern   success   accident

ace   face   race   space   lice   nice   rice   price   pence   office

Learner read:

✓✓   ✓✓   ✓✓   ✓✓

city	police	ace	cycle
except	rice	slice	dance
decide	success	parcel	cement
palace	fence	excite	force
price	twice	space	race
office	France	face	December
decent	recent	nice	Greece

Coach

soft c practice

Tick each sentence if all the words are right.

If your learner misreads a word, say it correctly, underline it, and move on.

After your learner has tried all the text, coach any underlined words.

Learner read:

The Cycle Race Accident

Last December an accident was reported in a French city.

Two cycles crashed during a cycle race in France.

The riders were from Greece.

The police came to the city centre to stop a fight.

One man who had been watching the race

hit one of the cycle aces with a fence post.

Another man threw a bag of rice at him.

The police had to step in twice.

One rider had to give up the race.

He had bad cuts on his face.

The other rider decided to set off again,

but success did not come his way.

He came in last.

Ace! .... is reading very nicely.

Reading for Fun

> If a man was born in Greece, grew up in Spain,
> came to England and died in France, what is he?
> Dead.
>
> Fun fact: The first cycle was made of wood.

Coach

oa (oh!)

Explain to your learner:
oa words like **coach** are pronounced like **oh** (surprise!).

At the top of the page, read each word to your learner,
then ask your learner to read it to you.

Below, tick every word read correctly.
If your learner misreads a word, correct it, underline, and move on.

After your learner has tried all the words, coach
any underlined words.

Repeat this page at the start of your next session.

Coach read each word, then learner read it:

coat   oats   boat   throat   goat   toad

poach   coach   boast   float   bloater   croak

Learner read:

✓✓   ✓✓   ✓✓   ✓✓

croak	foal	stoat	toad
coat	goat	bloater	oak
loaf	float	coach	oats
soap	road	throat	boast
poach	boat	goal	coast

Coach

oa practice

Tick each sentence if all the words are right.

If your learner misreads a word, say it correctly, underline it and move on.

After your learner has tried all the text, coach any underlined words.

Learner read:

✓ ✓

Croak! Croak! Croak! I can hear the frogs.

They sit on the lily pads floating in the pond.

Coach, can you hear the frogs croaking?

Yes, I can hear them croaking, but it may not be a frog.

It may be a toad croaking as it floats.

Toads croak too but toads don't like to be in the water.

So that is a frog with a croak in its throat.

This croaking is beginning to get my goat, so

come along, let's hit the road. Don't leave your coat.

Just coming, Coach!

.... has taken one more step along the road.

Reading for Fun

What do you call a vampire in a raincoat?
Mack u la.

What do you call a girl who lives on the same street as a vampire?
The girl necks door.

Fun fact: A cockroach can live for nine days without its head
before it starves to death.

Coach

ow (oh!)

There are two ways to read **ow**. Both ways crop up often.

Tell your learner -
ow words like **glow**, are pronounced **oh** (surprise!).

At the top of the page, read each word to your learner,
then ask your learner to read it to you.

Below, tick every word read correctly.
If your learner misreads a word, or hesitates, wait four seconds
then say the word correctly in a neutral voice. After your learner
has repeated the word correctly, underline it and move on.

After your learner has tried all the words, coach
any underlined words.

Repeat this page at the start of your next session.

Coach read each word, then learner read it:

glow	low	slow	blow	mow	snow
crow	flow	throw	grow	know	show

Learner read:

✓✓   ✓✓   ✓✓   ✓✓

show	know	snow	throw
below	low	shallow	elbow
borrow	slow	Glasgow	pillow
crow	blow	bow	narrow
shadow	grow	rainbow	window
follow	sparrow	yellow	grown-up

Coach

ow practice

Tick each sentence if all the words are right.

If your learner misreads a word, say it correctly, underline it and move on.

After your learner has tried all the text, coach any underlined words.

Learner read:

Let me show you my snow-man.

I know you will like it.

We have made a low fire near-by,

and it will give you a nice warm glow.

I fear the fire will slowly melt your snow-man.

Oh dear, you are right.

I was going to show you our snowman but

the fire has melted all the snow near it.

Still, the fire gives a warm glow.

Let's throw some more logs on it.

I'll show you where the trees grow,

so we can get more logs and twigs to throw on the fire.

Good, we know .... can read well.

Reading for Fun

What happens when you throw a yellow and brown rock
into a blue stream?
It makes a splash.

Coach and learner have a go at this tongue twister:
Three free throws, three free throws, three free throws.

Did you know? Polar bears are left-handed, and so are frogs.

Coach

oa and **ow** practice

Tick each sentence if all the words are right.

If your learner misreads a word, say it correctly, underline it and move on.

After your learner has tried all the text, coach any underlined words.

Joan and Billy Find a New Life

Long ago sailors kept goats on ships for fresh meat and milk. They were kept below deck, and were bred small to save room. Joan the nanny goat gave the sailors milk, but Billy her mate was going to be a fine goat stew one day soon.

Captain Boatman came below deck to look at his goats. "What a smell!" he bellowed. Billy liked the look of his red coat, so he began to chew it. Captain Boatman was filled with rage.

He grabbed Billy by the throat and threw him over the side of the ship. So Joan jumped in after her mate Billy. "Relax, take it slowly, we will swim for the land," said Joan.

A sheep was standing on the shore. "Welcome!" he said. "Come and live with us. We have loads of grass and plants growing here." After just a few years there were loads of small goats living on the island.

....................................'s **reading skills grow better every day.
Loads better!**

Coach

er

At the top of the page, read each word to your learner,
then ask your learner to read it to you.

Below, tick every word read correctly.
If your learner misreads a word, correct it, underline, and move on.

After your learner has tried all the words, coach
any underlined words.

Repeat this page at the start of your next session.

Coach read each word, then learner read it:

her   herb   stern   nerve   expert   silver

perhaps   father   mother   sister   brother

Learner read:

✓✓   ✓✓   ✓✓   ✓✓

her   stern   silver   mother

herb   expert   sister   brother

nerve   father   perhaps

Coach

er practice

Tick each sentence if all the words are right.

If your learner misreads a word, say it correctly, underline, and move on.

After your learner has tried all the text, coach
any underlined words.

Your learner is now ready to read **Snowball the Billy Goat** from our
range of reading books which support *Yes we can read.*

Learner read:

✓ ✓

My father drove my mother, my sister, my brother

and me to the sea-side.

"Look, there is a man with a herd of sheep," said my

brother Bert.

"No, you twerp, Bert, they are goats," said my sister Gerty.

My mother told my father to stop the car to ask the man

if his herd was goats or sheep.

"You ask him Herbert, I haven't got the nerve," said my

mother.

The man told us they were sheep who ate seaweed as

well as herbs and grass.

So my sister Gerty had to say sorry to my brother Bert for

calling him a twerp.

"Now perhaps we can drive on!" my father said.

.... **is becoming an expert at reading.**

Reading for Fun

What gets wetter as it is drying?
A towel.

Coach

ir pronounced **er**

Explain that **ir** as in **fir** makes the same sound as **er**.

At the top of the page, read each word to your learner,
then ask your learner to read it to you.

Below, tick every word read correctly.
If your learner misreads a word, or hesitates, wait four seconds
then say the word correctly in a neutral voice. After your learner
has repeated the word correctly, underline it and move on.

After your learner has tried all the words, coach
any underlined words.

Repeat this page at the start of your next session.

Coach read each word, then learner read it:

fir　　sir　　bird　　girl　　dirt　　birth　　shirt　　skirt

firm　　first　　third　　thirty　　thirteen　　circle

Learner read:

✓✓　　　✓✓　　　✓✓　　　✓✓

fir	dirt	firm	shirt
sir	girl	first	skirt
bird	birth	third	thirteen
thirty	circle	birthday	

Coach

ir practice

Tick each sentence if all the words are right.

If your learner misreads a word, say it correctly, underline, and move on.

After your learner has tried all the text, coach
any underlined words.

Learner read:

✓   ✓

Right boys and girls, form a circle.

I said, form a circle, a proper circle, not a big mess.

Sir, Sir, please Sir, that girl has got dirt on her skirt.

Hush up Birt, I am teaching about The Third Eye.

How old are you boy? Three or thirteen?

I am thirteen, Sir. It's my birthday today, Sir.

Well, well, thirteen. Happy birthday to you then, Birt.

Now let's get back to The Third Eye.

First of all I want you to turn to the first page in the book…

The bell has gone and I don't want all thirty of you

to leave at once. Boys stay. You girls go first.

You boy, tuck your shirt in.

That is the third time I have told you.

We must be firm about things like shirts.

……………………………………………. has a firm grip on reading now.

Reading for Fun

Why did the cat join the Red Cross?
She wanted to be a first-aid kit.

Why do cats chase birds?
For a lark.

Coach

ur pronounced **er**

Explain that **ur** as in **fur** makes the same sound as **er**.

At the top of the page, read each word to your learner,
then ask your learner to read it to you.

Below, tick every word read correctly.
If your learner misreads a word, or hesitates, wait four seconds
then say the word correctly in a neutral voice. After your learner
has repeated the word correctly, underline it and move on.

After your learner has tried all the words, coach
any underlined words.

Repeat this page at the start of your next session.

Coach read each word, then learner read it:

fur   burn   turn   curl   church   nurse   curve

hurt   curtain   Thursday   surprise   murder   urgent

Learner read:

✓✓   ✓✓   ✓✓   ✓✓

fur   turn   nurse   urgent

hurt   curl   murder   church

burn   curve   curtain   Thursday

surprise

Coach

ur practice

Tick each sentence if all the words are right.

If your learner misreads a word, say it correctly, underline, and move on.

After your learner has tried all the text, coach
any underlined words.

Learner read:

We are putting on a play in the church hall.

It is about a nurse who has a surprise.

I won't tell you the story, but there are a few murders.

I play the part of the nurse, who finds out who the

killer is, right at the end.

The curtain goes up on Thursday.

It is getting urgent for me to learn my lines.

I had better return to work, so that I know my lines when

the curtain goes up in the church hall on Thursday.

It is no surprise that .... reads well.

Reading for Fun

Why does a dog get so hot in the summer?
Because he wears a fur coat and pants.

Coach

er ir ur practice

Tick each sentence if all the words are right.

If your learner misreads a word, say it correctly, underline, and move on.

After your learner has tried all the text, coach
any underlined words.

Learner read:

✓   ✓

Hello Arthur, when is your birthday?

My birthday is on Thursday the third of June, Herby.

My twin brother and sister's birthday is on Thursday

the third of June too, and they will be thirteen.

Well Arthur, my birthday is on this coming Thursday, so

you will have to wish me a happy birthday before

your twin brother and sister.

It will be my thirty-first birthday.

I will have to see what I can get you for a surprise, Herby.

You don't need to give me a surprise for my birthday, Arthur.

I must say, I don't like surprises.

Many happy returns of the day will do, or perhaps you might

give me a card.

What about a trip to the circus, Herby?

.... **is further on.**

Coach

kn-

k is silent in front of **n**.

Tell your learner that **k** becomes silent in front of **n**,
as in **knock-knock**.

At the top of the page, read each word to your learner,
then ask your learner to read it to you.

Below, tick every word read correctly.
If your learner misreads a word, or hesitates, wait four seconds
then say the word correctly in a neutral voice. After your learner
has repeated the word correctly, underline it and move on.

After your learner has tried all the words, coach
any underlined words.

Tick each joke if all the words are right.
If your learner misreads a word, correct it, underline, and move on.

After your learner has tried all the jokes, coach
any underlined words.

Repeat this page at the start of your next session.

Coach read each word, then learner read it:

knee   knob   knots   knit   know   knew

knock   knocker   knife   knickers   knapsack

Learner read:

✓✓   ✓✓   ✓✓   ✓✓

knock   knee   know   knocker

knew   knots   knit   knapsack

knife   knob   knickers

Learner read the jokes:

✓✓   ✓✓

Knock-knock.   Knock-knock.

Who's there?   Who's there?

Boo.   Zizi.

Boo who?   Zizi who?

No need to cry. It's only a joke.   Zizi when you know how.

Knock-knock.   Knock-knock.

Who's there?   Who's there?

Dan.   Betty.

Dan who?   Betty who?

Dan Druff.   Betty things to do than

stand here, you know.

Do you know any better knock-knock jokes?

We all know .... reads well.

Reading for Fun

Coach and learner have a go at this tongue twister:
Knapsack straps, knapsack straps, knapsack straps.

Coach

wh-

h is silent after **w**.

Explain that **h** is silent after **w**, as in **white while whistle**.
We are adding to the question words, learned earlier:

  what   when   where   which   why

At the top of the page, read each word to your learner,
then ask your learner to read it to you.

Below, tick every word read correctly.
If your learner misreads a word, correct it, underline, and move on.

After your learner has tried all the words, coach
any underlined words.

Repeat this page at the start of your next session.

Coach read each word, then learner read it:

what   when   where   which   why   while

whizzing   white   whale   wheel   whisper   whopper

Learner read:

✓✓   ✓✓   ✓✓

when   which   why

white   while   whisper

what   where   wheel

whale   whopper   whizzing

Reading for Fun

Why do zebras like old films?
Because they are in black and white.

Fun fact: The heart of a blue whale is the size of a small car.

Coach

wh- practice

Tick each sentence if all the words are right.

If your learner misreads a word, say it correctly, underline it and move on.

After your learner has tried all the text, coach
any underlined words.

Learner read:

"Why, why, why is Leroy always, always late?"

my father said to my mother.

The three of us were sitting in our new white car, waiting

to take my brother to his football match.

Leroy's team was in the final after winning the last ten games.

At last he came whizzing up on his bicycle.

"Wow, whacky new wheels, Dad!" he said to my father, who

was drumming his fingers on the steering wheel.

"The whiff of the plastic seats makes me feel a bit sick,"

my mother whispered to me. "Don't tell your father!"

My brother made a great shot on goal, but

it whizzed past the posts, by a whisker.

In the last seconds of the game Leroy's winning goal

whizzed past the goalkeeper's ear into the net.

"Better late than never!" my mother whispered.

.... **has made whopping progress!**

Reading for Fun

> **Sea Fever - a poem by John Masefield**
>
> I must go down to the seas again, to the lonely sea and the sky,
> And all I ask is a tall ship and a star to steer her by,
> And the wheel's kick and the wind's song and the white sail's shaking,
> And a grey mist on the sea's face and a grey dawn breaking.
>
> I must go down to the seas again, for the call of the running tide
> Is a wild call and a clear call that may not be denied;
> And all I ask is a windy day with the white clouds flying,
> And the flung spray and the blown spume, and the sea-gulls crying.

Coach

ow (painful!)

Tell your learner the other way to read **ow** -
        ow as in **cow** makes the sound **ow** (that hurts!).

At the top of the page, read each word to your learner,
then ask your learner to read it to you.

Below, tick every word read correctly.
If your learner misreads a word, correct it, underline, and move on.

After your learner has tried all the words, coach
any underlined words.

Tick each sentence if all the words are right.
If your learner misreads a word, correct it, underline, and move on.

After your learner has tried all the sentences, coach
any underlined words.

Repeat this page at the start of your next session.

Coach read each word, then learner read it:

cow   how   crown   flower   powder

down   owl   now   fowl   bow-wow

Learner read:

✓✓   ✓✓   ✓✓

cow	owl	fowl
now	down	crown
how	powder	flower

Learner read:

✓   ✓

How now, brown cow?

Now Daisy the cow is going to the fair.

I think Daisy the cow will win a prize today.

So you think that Daisy will win the brown cow crown,

and that we will shower her with flowers if she wins.

Yes, but what sort of flowers shall we shower her with?

Cowslips, I suppose.

This is silly. Our cow may not win now. There will be

lots of cows down at the fair that might beat our cow

and win the prize.

Now, ... , how's that? Wow!

Reading for Fun

If cows talk all at once what do they say?
Nothing. Cows don't talk.

Coach

ou (painful!)

Tell your learner that **ou** as in **out** makes
the same sound as **ow** (that hurts!).

At the top of the page, read each word to your learner,
then ask your learner to read it to you.

Below, tick every word read correctly.
If your learner misreads a word, correct it, underline, and move on.

After your learner has tried all the words, coach
any underlined words.

Tick each sentence if all the words are right.
If your learner misreads a word, correct it, underline, and move on.

After your learner has tried all the sentences, coach
any underlined words.

Repeat this page at the start of your next session.

Coach read each word, then learner read it:

out	our	round	house	loud
count	sound	mouse	fountain	mountain

Learner read:

✓✓   ✓✓   ✓✓

out	round	count
our	house	mouse
loud	sound	mountain

Learner read:

✓   ✓

Captain the cat is chasing a huge mouse around our house.

It may be a rat! Don't be silly, you are making a mountain

out of a molehill. It is just a mouse.

I am afraid of mice and that mouse is loose around our house.

Do you have to shout so loud?

I will throw the mouse outside the house.

Count one, two, three, and I will catch the mouse.

There you are, all gone!

Let's give Captain his clockwork mouse to play with.

Wow .... ! How about that!

Reading for Fun

What's striped and bouncy?
A tiger on a pogo stick.

Which animal should need oil?
A mouse, because it squeaks.

What is the loudest pet?
A trum..pet.

Did you know? A house fly can only live for fourteen days.

Coach

ow and **ou** practice

Tick each sentence if all the words are right.

If your learner misreads a word, or hesitates, wait four seconds
then say the word correctly in a neutral voice. After your learner
has repeated the word correctly, underline it and move on.

After your learner has tried all the text, coach
any underlined words.

Learner read:

I found my kite and went out, and down to Howard's house.

"Wow!" said Howard, "Let's go round to the park."

I let out the strings as Howard walked backwards,

counting up to twenty. "Shall I throw it up now?"

"Yes, now!" I shouted, loudly.

He threw the kite high in the air. Whoosh!

It tugged on the strings and rose higher and higher.

"Wow! How about trying to hit the clouds!"

I let out more string but the kite turned round and

whizzed down to the ground, crashing into the flowers.

Wow! That was good work.

.... has found out how to crack reading.

Coach

Look Write Say

One more batch of words that **don't follow easy rules**
and have to be learned by the *Look Write Say* method.

In the top line, point at any word and read it, then ask your learner
to read the word to you.
Don't read the letters separately - **say the whole word** - because
your learner is **MEMORISING the SHAPE of the WHOLE WORD**.

Make sure you cover each word at least twice.

Ask your learner to read you the words in the next section, unprompted.
Tick correct words, otherwise wait four seconds and say
the word correctly, then underline it.

Coach any underlined words.

> If your learner still has difficulty with a word, write it on a piece
>
> of spare paper, saying the word as you write.
>
> Then ask your learner to copy your word, up to ten times,
>
> saying the word as they are writing it.
>
> **This is a useful technique for any word**
>
> **your learner struggles with, now or later.**

Ask your learner to read each sentence to you, then either tick it
or correct any misread words and underline them.

After your learner has tried all the sentences, coach
any underlined words.

Repeat this page at the start of your next session.

Coach point to a word and read it, then learner read it:

once	world	because	eight	eighty
could	would	should	school	

Learner read:

✓✓   ✓✓   ✓✓

once	could	eight
world	eighty	would
should	because	school

Learner read sentences:

✓   ✓

How many holes has your golf club got?

It has eighteen holes.

Did you say eight?

No, eighteen, you nit!

Could I join your golf club?

No. You would not be able to join, because

you don't know how to play.

I did play once, eight years ago.

You should have lessons at the golf school, because

then you would see if you want to play.

I think it's the best game in the world!

I know it is.

We should all say .... is a star.

195

Coach

aw (what a shame!)

At the top of the page, read each word to your learner,
then ask your learner to read it to you.

Below, tick every word read correctly.
If your learner misreads a word, correct it, underline, and move on.

After your learner has tried all the words, coach
any underlined words.

Tick each sentence if all the words are right.
If your learner misreads a word, correct it, underline, and move on.

After your learner has tried all the sentences, coach
any underlined words.

Repeat this page at the start of your next session.

Tip

> Show your learner the names of shops, food outlets, streets, towns
> or other places your learner knows. The ability to read difficult words
> will increase your learner's confidence.
> One of our teenage learners couldn't read burger, double, cheese or
> fries until he finished the book. But he could read the three-syllable
> name of the worldwide food outlets that sold them.

Coach read each word, then learner read it:

    paw   law   saw   raw   jaw

    draw   prawn   straw   crawl

Learner read:

✓✓   ✓✓   ✓✓

jaw	raw	prawn
law	saw	crawl
paw	draw	straw

Learner read:

✓   ✓

My dog Paws and I went to catch some prawns in the rock pools.

My mother-in-law was coming for lunch. She loves fresh prawns.

I had a big bag full of prawns, when I saw

poor Paws was limping and holding up his paw.

"Aw, poor Paws!" I said. He started to whimper softly.

My friend Dawn saw that Paws had a crab claw stuck in his paw.

Dawn took the crab claw out of his paw, and he crawled off.

In next to no time his paw was better and

he ran off to chase the crabs and gulls again.

Awesome! ....'s progress is jaw-dropping.

Reading for Fun

What did the cat say when she lost all her money?
"I'm paw."

Fun fact: A prawn's heart is in its head.

Coach

Longer words

Your learner may find the prospect of longer words threatening.
It is important to say that reading long words is going to be easy.

Longer words are made up of syllables (word parts).

A syllable is a beat in a word - you can hear it, and
you can feel it by putting the back of your hand
under your chin as you speak a word.

Every syllable contains just one vowel-sound -
that can be the sound of just one vowel - **con**
or a blend of vowels that make one sound - **tains**

Deal with one word at a time.

Cover up the word with a piece of paper or your forefinger.
Move it to the right, revealing one syllable at a time.
Then ask your learner to read the unsplit word.

Next time you move down the words, ask your learner to read
each line unprompted. Tick every line read correctly.
If your learner misreads a word, correct it, underline, and move on.

After your learner has tried all the words, coach
any underlined words.

Repeat this page at the start of your next session.

Coach cover each word, then uncover it, bit by bit . . .

Learner read:
✓ ✓

fan tas tic	fantastic
mar vell ous	marvellous
a ma zing	amazing
out stan ding	outstanding
mag ni fi cent	magnificent
ex cell ent	excellent
fa bu lous	fabulous
fan ta bu lous	fantabulous
glor i ous	glorious
splen did	splendid
yab ba dab ba doo	yabba-dabba-doo

Learner read:

Good! I have made excellent progress with my reading.
Yes, you certainly have.

Reading for Fun

> Why was six so afraid of seven?
> Seven eight nine.
> (Seven ate nine.)

Coach

reading practice

Tick each sentence if all the words are right.

If your learner misreads a word, say it correctly . . .

      then cover up the word and reveal each syllable, one at a time.
      This will help your learner to identify separate syllables,
      pronounce each syllable on its own and then
      say them once again, running the syllables together . . .

and then underline the word and move on.

After your learner has tried all the text, coach
any underlined words.

Learner read:

✓   ✓

Those wheels are awe some. Yes they are awesome.
Do you want to have a go on my awesome wheels?

It is a fan tas tic day today. Why is it fantastic?
Spring has come, the sun is shining, so it's a fantastic day.

You have made ex cell ent progress with your reading.
Do you mean excellent progress? Yes I do mean excellent.

What a mag ni fi cent horse! Yes it is magnificent.
It is the most magnificent horse I've seen. He ran an
out stan ding race. Yes it was outstanding. Outstanding!

You are having a baby! That's mar vell ous news.
Yes it's marvellous news, just marvellous news.

That was a splen did meal. Thank you. I am glad you think
it was splendid. Yes I do, I think it was splendid.

Yogi Bear said yab ba dab ba doo. No, it wasn't Yogi
Bear who said yabba-dabba-doo, it was Popeye who said
yabba-dabba-doo. I know, it was Fred Flintstone who said
yabba-dabba-doo. Well, yabba-dabba-doo to you too.

.... **has made excellent progress.**

Coach

more **Longer words**

Here are some more words to help your learner's new-found skills become embedded.

Reassure your learner that they can read any long word.

It may help to remind them:
every syllable contains just one vowel-sound, and
you can feel each syllable by putting the back of your hand
under your chin when you speak a word.

Deal with one word at a time.
Cover up the word with a piece of paper or your forefinger.
Move it to the right, revealing one syllable at a time.
Then ask your learner to read the unsplit word.

Next time you move down the list, ask your learner to read
each line unprompted. Tick every line read correctly.
If your learner misreads a word, correct it, underline, and move on.

After your learner has tried all the words, coach
any underlined words.

Repeat this page at the start of your next session.

Coach cover each word, then uncover it, bit by bit . . .

Learner read:
✓   ✓

aw ful	awful
dis gus ting	disgusting
fright ful	frightful
dread ful	dreadful
re vol ting	revolting
horr en dous	horrendous
dis grace ful	disgraceful
re pell ent	repellent
hate ful ness	hatefulness
smell i ness	smelliness
terr i fy ing	terrifying

That was not too difficult. I feel more confident now.

Well done .... You are a star!

Coach

reading practice

Tick each sentence if all the words are right.

If your learner misreads a word, say it correctly . . .

      then cover up the word and reveal each syllable, one at a time.
      This will help your learner to identify separate syllables,
      pronounce each syllable on its own and then
      say them once again, running the syllables together . . .

and then underline the word and move on.

After your learner has tried all the text, coach
any underlined words.

Repeat this page at the start of your next session.

Tip

> Read an exciting book together. Books for new readers are called
> New or Quick or Easy or Beginner Readers (you will find some great
> ones at www.gatehousebooks.com).
> When you reach an exciting, cliff-hanger part, put the book down,
> saying you have to go, and leave it for your learner to pick up and
> read without you there. One of our learners who swore she would
> never be able to read a book demanded a second one as soon
> as she had finished the 'hook-book'.

Learner read:

✓   ✓

I have an aw ful pain in my foot. An awful pain in your tooth?
No, I have an awful pain in my foot.

This smell is dis gus ting. Which smell is disgusting?
The smell of rotting fish is disgusting.

Your room is a fright ful mess. My room is not a frightful
mess. I like it that way. I'm telling you, it's a frightful mess.

The plane crash was horr en dous. Yes, it was horrendous,
really horrendous.

I find the smell of dog-poo re pell ent. I find the smell of
cat-poo repellent. I find the smell of any poo repellent.

No more talk of smell i ness please.
Smelliness? I agree, no more talk of smelliness.

I hate all this hate ful ness. Yes I hate all this hatefulness.
I think hatefulness is, well, hateful.

That horror film was terr i fy ing. Well, I don't think it
was so terrifying. It was too silly to be really terrifying.

Was that difficult?

.... **is even more confident now. What a star!**

Coach

reading practice

Tick each sentence if all the words are right.

If your learner misreads a word, say it correctly . . .

      then cover up the word and reveal each syllable, one at a time.
      This will help your learner to identify separate syllables,
      pronounce each syllable on its own and then
      say them once again, running the syllables together . . .

and then underline the word and move on.

After your learner has tried all the text, coach
any underlined words.

Newsflash

A Greek oil tanker has sunk off the coast of Spain,

spilling over fifty thousand tons of oil into the sea.

The lovely beaches are now a disgusting sight

and the smell of dead fish is revolting.

The number of dead seagulls is horrendous.

"It is horrible to think how many more birds and

sea animals will die," said Costas, a local fisherman.

"It's awful, just awful," sobbed Elena, his wife,

"and the smelliness and repellent sight of the

dead birds and fish will turn holidaymakers away.

It is terrifying to think what will happen to us all."

Well done .... That is lovely.

Coach

'-shn' add-ons

Words like sta**tion**   musi**cian**   ten**sion**   se**ssion**
are all pronounced **-shn** at the end.

Your learner should soon get used to recognising these syllables
at the end of a word, or near to the end of it.

Deal with one word at a time.
Cover up the word with a piece of paper or your forefinger.
Move it to the right, revealing one syllable at a time.
Then ask your learner to read the unsplit word.

Next time you move down the columns, ask your learner to read
each pair unprompted. Tick every pair read correctly.
If your learner misreads a word, correct it, underline, and move on.

After your learner has tried all the pairs, coach
any underlined words.

Repeat this page at the start of your next session.

You may deem it necessary to repeat this exercise several times.

Coach cover each word, then uncover it, bit by bit as learner reads:

✓✓   ✓✓

sta tion	station	per fec tion	perfection
frac tion	fraction	mus i cian	musician
ques tion	question	op ti cian	optician
mo tion	motion	pol i ti cian	politician
ten sion	tension	in di ges tion	indigestion
ver sion	version	pre scrip tion	prescription
pen sion	pension	gen er a tion	generation
e mo tion	emotion	se ssion	session
com pe ti tion	competition	pa ssion	passion
in form a tion	information	con fe ssion	confession
sen sa tion	sensation	dis cu ssion	discussion
re cep tion	reception	ex pre ssion	expression

...................................'s reading progress is sensational!
Yes, there is no question about it.

Coach

reading practice

Your learner should continue to gain confidence from being able to
read different kinds of longer words.

Ask your learner to read the story to you.
Tick each sentence if all the words are right.

If your learner misreads a word, say it correctly . . .

    then cover up the word and reveal each syllable, one at a time.
    This will help your learner to identify separate syllables,
    pronounce each syllable on its own and then
    say them once again, running the syllables together . . .

and then underline the word and move on.

After your learner has tried all the text, coach
any underlined words.

Learner read:

The stationmaster shouted over the loudspeaker:

"Attention! Attention! The train from Queenstown will arrive one hour late. There has been an accident on the line."

He repeated himself:

"Attention! Attention! The train from Queenstown will be arriving one hour late. There has been an accident."

"What a frightful bore!" drawled the posh man who was standing next to me on the platform.

"We might as well go and have a cup of tea," I said to the posh man. He looked at me for a fraction of a second.

"Yes, but I have a confession to make. I haven't got any cash on me."

"Never mind, I'll buy you one," I said. "May I ask a question? Why haven't you got any money on you?"

"Good question," he said. "My wallet was stolen just outside the station."

Sensational, ... !

Reading for Fun

> What question can you never answer yes to?
> Are you asleep?
>
> Did you know?
> Every year more than a hundred million books
> are stolen from book shops in Britain.

Coach

-le

-le (at the end of a word) is pronounced as **l**.

Words like **middle**, **uncle**, **puzzle** end in a soft **l** sound.

At the top of the page, read each word to your learner,
then ask your learner to read it to you.

Below, tick every paragraph read correctly.
If your learner misreads a word, correct it, underline, and move on.

After your learner has tried all the paragraphs, coach
any underlined words.

Repeat this page at the start of your next session.

Coach read each word, then learner read it,

then both think up rhymes for each word:

pimple	middle	grumble	uncle
eagle	puzzle	handle	cattle

Learner read:

In the middle of the little table was a single apple, next to the candle-stick with the handle. My uncle took the apple. He had a struggle to reach it, but it was not impossible.

It is such a fiddle threading this needle, I think I will go and get my spectacles.

Here is a little puzzle to make you think a little:

Question: Six women are in a huddle under one umbrella. Why do they all stay dry?

Answer: It is not raining.

That was hard work,

but perhaps you had a little bit of a giggle.

.... **can handle difficult stuff.**

Reading for Fun

What did one candle say to the other candle?
"Are you going out tonight?"

Fun fact: It is impossible to sneeze with your eyes open.

Coach

Riddles

You may be familiar with the riddles, but please encourage your learner to work out the answers.

(The answers are at the bottom of your learner's page.)

Tick each riddle if all the words are right.

If your learner misreads a word, or hesitates, wait four seconds then say the word correctly in a neutral voice. After your learner has repeated the word correctly, underline it and move on.

After your learner has tried all the riddles, coach any underlined words.

Learner read the riddles to your coach, and then together work out the answers. (The answers are below.)

✓✓ Riddle number 1

You and your coach are lost and alone in the middle of the woods. You stumble across a little cabin and decide to stay there for the night. You want some heat and light, but the only things you find in the cabin are a candle, an oil lamp and a wood burning stove. You look in your pockets but you only have one match left. What do you light first?

✓✓ Riddle number 2

What was the highest mountain before Mount Everest was discovered?

✓✓ Riddle number 3

I sizzle like bacon. I am made with an egg.
I have plenty of backbone, but lack a good leg.
What am I?

✓✓ Riddle number 4

A woman has seven children, and half of them are boys.
How is this possible?

✓✓ Riddle number 5

A pet shop owner said, "This lovely purple parrot will repeat every word it hears, and that is no idle promise." A man took the bird home, but it would not say a single word.
Nevertheless the salesman was speaking the truth.
How was this possible?

.... **can handle reading and riddles.**

Answers: 1: the match. 2: Mount Everest. 3: a snake.
4: all of the children are boys, so half of them are boys.
5: the purple parrot was deaf.

Coach

ph

ph is pronounced as **f**.
Philip   physics   orphan   nephew
. . . and **photograph** does it at both ends.

At the top of the page, read each word to your learner,
then ask your learner to read it to you.

Below, tick every word read correctly.
If your learner misreads a word, correct it, underline, and move on.

After your learner has tried all the words, coach
any underlined words.

Tick each paragraph if all the words are right.
If your learner misreads a word, correct it, underline, and move on.

After your learner has tried all the paragraphs, coach
any underlined words.

Repeat this page at the start of your next session.

Coach read each word, then learner:

photo   phoney   elephant   phantom   telephone   nephew

phonic   phone   orphan   alphabet   physics   Philippa

Learner read:

✓✓   ✓✓   ✓✓   ✓✓

photo   phone   elephant   phantom

Philip   alphabet   phoney   physics

orphan   phonic   nephew   telephone

Learner read:

 ✓✓

I have a photo of my nephew and his best mate.
The photograph shows my nephew and his friend.
His friend is called Philip and he is an orphan.
His mother was a physics teacher.

We use the phonic alphabet to learn to read. That means we
call letters by their sounds, and not by their alphabet names.

I tend to use my mobile more than the house telephone.
My friends and I are thinking of getting rid of the house phone
and just using our mobile phones.

My friend wants to take me to see The Phantom Of The
Opera as a treat for my birthday, but I don't want to see
The Phantom because I don't like musicals.

Phew! Made it! No more for today!

.... **has made phenomenal progress.**

Reading for Fun

Did you know?
Elephants and sloths are the only animals that can't jump.

Coach

ph practice

Knock-knock jokes for names with **ph**
are especially dreadful, so grit your teeth for a
groan-groan session.

Tick each joke if all the words are right.

If your learner misreads a word, say it correctly, underline it and move on.

After your learner has tried all the jokes, coach
any underlined words.

Learner read:

The knock-knock jokes for names with **ph** are really lame.
Do you or your friends know any better ones?

✓✓ Knock-knock who's there?
Philip.
Philip who?
Philip the gas tank. I'm running low.

✓✓ Knock-knock who's there?
Stephanie.
Stephanie who?
Stephanie gas pedal. We are running late.

✓✓ Knock-knock who's there?
Rain.
Rain who?
Rudolph, the red nose reindeer.

✓✓ Knock-knock who's there?
Adolph.
Adolph who?
Adolph ball hit me in the mouth.

✓✓ Knock-knock who's there?
Ralph.
Ralph who?
Ralph, Ralph, Ralph, your little puppy.

Groan, groan! Those jokes were really awful.
Let's have no more knock-knock jokes.

.... **has cracked it!**

Coach

-gh (at the end of a word) can be silent or can be pronounced **f**.

-gh when pronounced **f**

Tell your learner -
Here are some words ending with **-gh** when it's pronounced **f**.

At the top of the page, read each word to your learner,
then ask your learner to read it to you.

Your learner has to memorise the shapes of these words,
so you should go through this exercise together several times.

Below, tick every word read correctly.
If your learner misreads a word, correct it, underline, and move on.

After your learner has tried all the words, coach
any underlined words.

Tick each sentence if all the words are right.
If your learner misreads a word, correct it, underline, and move on.

After your learner has tried all the sentences, coach
any underlined words.

Repeat this page at the start of your next session.

Coach read:

In these words ending with **-gh**, the **-gh** is pronounced **-f**.

Coach read each word, then learner read it:

tough   rough   enough   laugh   cough

Learner read:

✓✓   ✓✓   ✓✓   ✓✓   ✓✓

cough   laugh   rough   tough   enough

Learner read:

✓✓

Cindy is sixty-one years old, and she has had a tough life.

She didn't learn to read until she was sixty.

It was rough and very tough for her,

but now she can laugh about it.

She did not think she was clever enough to learn to read.

Her coach and this book showed her that she was

more than clever enough.

Now her life has changed so much.

She can read books and letters, and she can read the

words all around her - in the home, in the shops and in

all of the outside world.

.... **has learnt some tough words today.**

221

Coach

-gh when **silent**

Tell your learner -
Here are some words ending with **-gh** when it is **silent**.

At the top of the page, read each word to your learner,
then ask your learner to read it to you.

Your learner has to memorise the shapes of these words,
so you should go through this exercise together several times.

Below, tick every word read correctly.
If your learner misreads a word, correct it, underline, and move on.

After your learner has tried all the words, coach
any underlined words.

Tick each sentence if all the words are right.
If your learner misreads a word, correct it, underline, and move on.

After your learner has tried all the sentences, coach
any underlined words.

Repeat this page at the start of your next session.

Your learner is now ready to read **Dog Heroes** from our range of
reading books which support *Yes we can read.*

Coach read:

In **these** words ending with **-gh**, the **-gh** is **silent**.

Coach read each word, then learner read it:

though   although   dough   borough   thorough   through

Learner read:

though	through	although
borough	dough	thorough

Learner read:

Although Delroy is very smart and funny, he has been through a hard time at school. Other kids made fun of him because of his reading. But he and his coach have been through the book, and now he can cope with school.

He can read anything and likes comics, although he still doesn't read books just for fun. His mother is thoroughly proud of him, and he can be thoroughly proud of himself.

.... **has been through some hard reading.**

Coach

-ght always pronounced **t**

Tell your learner -
Here are some words ending with **-ght**, always pronounced **t**.

At the top of the page, read each word to your learner,
then ask your learner to read it to you.

Your learner has to memorise the shapes of these words,
so you should go through this exercise together several times.

Below, tick every word read correctly.
If your learner misreads a word, correct it, underline, and move on.

After your learner has tried all the words, coach
any underlined words.

Tick each sentence if all the words are right.
If your learner misreads a word, correct it, underline, and move on.

After your learner has tried all the sentences, coach
any underlined words.

Repeat this page at the start of your next session.

Coach read:

Words ending with **-ght** are pronounced **-t.**

Coach read each word, then learner read it:

ought   fought   bought   brought   thought   caught

taught   naughty   daughter   height   weight

Learner read:

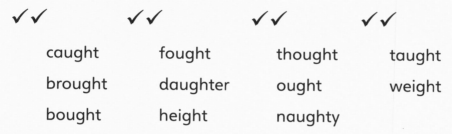

caught   fought   thought   taught

brought   daughter   ought   weight

bought   height   naughty

Learner read:

Jade is seventeen, and she has a baby girl. No-one taught

Jade to read at school. She thought she would never learn

to read. When she had brought her daughter into the world

Jade thought she ought to learn, so that she could read to her

daughter and show her how to read. As soon as Jade started

the **Yes we can read** book, she caught on very quickly. Now

she feels she is pulling her weight as a mother, because she

reads to her baby daughter every night.

We ought to give .... **a big clap.**

Coach

-gh practice

Tick each sentence if all the words are right.

If your learner misreads a word, or hesitates, wait four seconds then say the word correctly in a neutral voice. After your learner has repeated the word correctly, underline it and move on.

After your learner has tried all the text, coach
any underlined words.

Learner read:

My naughty daughter was asked to leave the musical,
The Phantom Of The Opera, because my naughty
daughter went cough cough, all the way through.

My teacher is a good laugh. Yes she is a good laugh,
but she is very thorough when it comes to revision,
very thorough indeed.

We hacked our way through the jungle although
the going was rough, really rough. It was very tough,
very tough indeed.

I think we have done enough work for today
and I think we ought to stop right now.

Could you read just a bit more?
No! I thought I said we have done enough work
for today and I think we ought to stop, now.
Enough is enough, I say!

.... **has made a big breakthrough.**

Reading for Fun

What did the lioness say to her cubs when she
taught them to be good lions?
"Don't go over the road till you see the zebra crossing."

Coach and learner have a go at this tongue twister:
I thought a thought, but the thought I thought
wasn't the thought I thought I thought.

Did you know?
The ant can lift fifty times its own weight.
Most elephants weigh less than the tongue of the blue whale.
The mosquito causes more human deaths than any other animal.

Coach

plural of **-y**

Nouns which end in **-y**
become, in the plural, **-ies** pronounced with a long **e**.
e.g. **baby** becomes **babies**.

Ask your learner to read the pairs.

Tick every word pair read correctly.
If your learner misreads a word, correct it, underline, and move on.

After your learner has tried all the words, coach
any underlined words.

Tick each sentence if all the words are right.
If your learner misreads a word, correct it, underline, and move on.

After your learner has tried all the sentences, coach
any underlined words.

Coach and learner read:

When there is more than one of a thing ending **-y**, it becomes **-ies**.

Learner read:

✓✓

one	more than one
baby	babies
pony	ponies
belly	bellies
penny	pennies
bunny	bunnies
nappy	nappies
puppy	puppies
poppy	poppies
copy	copies
lady	ladies
duty	duties
lolly	lollies
dolly	dollies
rally	rallies

Learner read:

✓✓

The babies had their smelly nappies changed again.

Most people like babies and puppies.

The pony ate the poppies and felt very sleepy.

The lady stroked the ponies.

The puppy licked the ice-lollies.

Billy the bully called the weenies "wallies" and "ninnies".

He gives me the willies.

The soldier carries out his duties.

.... **carries on making huge progress.**

Coach

reading practice

Tick each sentence if all the words are right.

If your learner misreads a word, say it correctly, underline it and move on.

After your learner has tried all the text, coach any underlined words.

Learner read:

Bringing Up Babies

Most people will be involved with babies at some point in their lives, so there really ought to be more advice and teaching for everyone. Many children may help to bring up younger brothers and sisters, or they could come into contact with babies through baby-sitting, when they become teenagers. Parents and grandparents would benefit from being taught more about the latest developments.

Although there are health visitors and clinics for expectant and new parents, that can never be enough. For instance, in years gone by, parents were told they should never put dummies in babies' mouths. Then parents were told to use them, because new research had shown that dummies could prevent cot death.

We should all give as much attention as possible to babies, and we should talk to them, play with them and read to them as early as possible. Although they may not be able to speak yet at this stage, their brains are growing very fast. Babies take in far more than we can know. But most of all they need love and laughter. Schools ought to teach their students how to look after a baby. Well, it's a thought, anyway.

Tough stuff, ... !

Reading for Fun

Fun facts:
The giraffe cleans its own ears with its very long tongue!
The giraffe's tongue is black.
Coffee beans are the seeds of a cherry tree.
There are 22 bones in your head.
A crocodile cannot stick its tongue out.
The can opener was invented forty-eight years after
cans were introduced to people! Think about it!

Coach

ie and **ei**

ie and **ei** are pronounced as a **long e** sound.

You may remember from school the spelling rule,
i before **e** except after **c**,

however, for your learner to read words like achieve and receive
it is best to follow our usual methods.

At the top of the page, point to each word and read it to your
learner, then ask your learner to read it to you.
Your learner has to memorise the shapes of these words,
so you should go through this exercise together several times.

Below, tick every word read correctly.
If your learner misreads a word, correct it, underline, and move on.
After your learner has tried all the words, coach
any underlined words.

Tick each sentence if all the words are right.
If your learner misreads a word, correct it, underline, and move on.
After your learner has tried all the sentences, coach
any underlined words.

Repeat this page at the start of your next session.

Coach read each word, then learner:

chief   relief   thief   belief   piece   field   receipt
believe   receive   achieve   deceive   ceiling   mischief

Learner read:

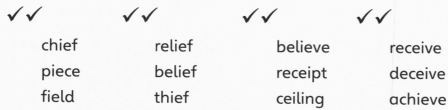

chief	relief	believe	receive
piece	belief	receipt	deceive
field	thief	ceiling	achieve

Learner read:

In the supermarket I asked for a receipt for the shopping, but then I dropped the receipt. So now I have lost my receipt.

We walked across the fields for a picnic in the woods, to get some relief from all the traffic. The traffic was so loud. What a relief! In the field I ate a piece of cake.

"I don't want to deceive you," said the chief to his staff. "You'll all have to work overtime, but you will not receive extra pay." "That is not fair," the foreman said to the chief. "It is my belief that if we work overtime, we should receive extra pay." "I don't care what you believe. Times are hard," said the chief. "This time you will receive no extra pay."

"It is amazing what you have achieved," the coach said to the learner. "I would never have believed that you could achieve so much. What an achievement!"

We ought to give .... a big clap.

Reading for Fun

> Coach and learner have a go at this tongue twister:
> Thieves seize skis, thieves seize skis, thieves seize skis.

Coach

ps-

ps- words have a silent **p**.
They are difficult to read, until your learner gets into the habit of ignoring
the **p** . . .

psalm   psychology   pseud   psychedelic

Fortunately there are not many and they are not common words.
With the **psych-** words your learner also has to learn to
ignore the **h** in **ch**, i.e. pronounce the **ch** as a hard **c**.

So **ps-** is a *Look Write Say* area.

Your learner should take great pride in being able to read some of the
most difficult words in English.

At the top of the page, point to each word and read it to your
learner, and ask your learner to read it to you.

Your learner has to memorise the shapes of these words,
so you should go through this exercise together several times.

Below, tick every word read correctly.
If your learner misreads a word, correct it, underline, and move on.

After your learner has tried all the words, coach
any underlined words.

Tick each sentence if all the words are right.
If your learner misreads a word, correct it, underline, and move on.

After your learner has tried all the sentences, coach
any underlined words.

Repeat this page at the start of your next session.

Coach read each word, then learner:

psycho   pseud   psychology   psychedelic   psychiatrist

Learner read:

✓✓   ✓✓   ✓✓

psycho   psychosis   psychology

psychedelic   psychiatrist   pseud

Learner read:

✓✓

Psycho is a very creepy old film.
It was made in the early sixties.

In the sixties, hippies wore flowers in their hair
and talked about peace and love.
The men had long hair down to their shoulders.
The women, and the men, wore psychedelic colours.
Today the hippie movement may all seem a bit pseud.

"I have studied psychology for years and years,
and I still don't understand women,"
said the psychiatrist, "and I am one!"

.... can read the hardest words.

Reading for Fun

Did you know?

Discombobulate means to upset:
"Grumpy is in a bad mood, so don't discombobulate him!"
The banana is a herb, and the tomato is a fruit.
Carrots have zero fat content.
China uses forty-five billion chopsticks a year.
The made-up word supercallifragilisticexpialidocious
comes from a song in the film Mary Poppins.

Coach

wr-

wr- words have a **silent w**.
They are hard to read until your learner gets into the habit of ignoring
the **w**.

Some of these are quite common words, so in the course of everyday
reading, your learner will soon ignore the **w** automatically.

At the top of the page, read each word to your learner,
then ask your learner to read it to you.

You should go through these words, randomly, at least twice.

Below, tick every word read correctly.
If your learner misreads a word, correct it, underline, and move on.

After your learner has tried all the words, coach
any underlined words.

Tick each sentence if all the words are right.
If your learner misreads a word, correct it, underline, and move on.

After your learner has tried all the sentences, coach
any underlined words.

Repeat this page at the start of your next session.

Coach read each word, then learner:

wrong   write   writer   wriggle   wren   wreck

wrench   wrinkle   wrap   wretch   wreath   wrestle

Learner read:

✓✓   ✓✓   ✓✓   ✓✓

wrong	write	wriggle	wreck
wrench	wrap	wreath	wrist
writer	wren	wrestle	wrinkle

Learner read:

✓✓

Here is some writing about the wreckfish.

The wreckfish lives down at the bottom of the sea. It can be as long as two metres. It can weigh as much as a hundred kilos. So you wouldn't want to wrestle with one.

It is found on the sea bed looking for food as it glides and wriggles its way through underwater caves and the wrecks of old ships - which is how it got its name, wreckfish.

Let's write it again, ... is a star reader.

Coach

other **silent** letters

Ask your reader to read these sentences
. . . which all contain words with a silent letter.

Then ask your reader to underline the silent letters.

Congratulations to you both!

Reader read each sentence...

then underline the silent letters in the **bold** words:

My friend and I **often** go to see Nelson's **column**.

When you are making fried eggs, try not to break the egg **yolks**.

I got the date **wrong**. Our meeting was on **Wednesday**.

I washed my shirt. Now I need to **iron** it.

Listen! It must be spring. The **lambs** are bleating.

When I saw the **ghost**, I **gnawed** my **knuckles** in terror.

Should '**rhyme**' rhyme with 'time'?

Who wrote "The **Sword** In The Stone"?

Please give me the **whole answer**. I **know** you **know** it.

The world of **science** has a **rhythm** all of its own.

The **plumber** got his **thumb** stuck in the spout of the tap.

I feel **calm** about reading now, and that is a good **sign**.

Yes, we can read!

Coach and Reader,

both of you may find these quotes (from the Internet) interesting and encouraging. Every one of these famous people has dyslexia.

Meg Matthews

I hated school and felt really held back by my dyslexia.

Orlando Bloom

I fell in love with Drama at school but struggled with other lessons because of my dyslexia.

Richard Branson

Being dyslexic can actually help in the outside world. I see some things clearer than other people do because I have to simplify things to help me and that helps others.

Tom Cruise

Being dyslexic I had to train myself to focus my attention. I became very visual and learned how to create mental images in order to comprehend what I read.

Winston Churchill

I was on the whole considerably discouraged by my school days. It was not pleasant to feel oneself so completely outclassed and left behind at the beginning of the race.

Jamie Oliver

It was with great regret that I didn't do better at school. People just thought I was thick. It was a struggle.

Jerry Hall

I am dyslexic and so are four of my children. It can be very difficult at the beginning but then you can learn to cope with it.

Albert Einstein's schoolteacher

Young Einstein was mentally slow, unsociable and adrift forever in his foolish dreams.

. . . and on the opposite page are the names of some of the many many famous people who have dyslexia.

Actors & Entertainers

Marlon Brando, Orlando Bloom, Tom Cruise, Harrison Ford, Johnny Depp, Whoopi Goldberg, Eddie Izzard, Harry Belafonte, Danny Glover, Susan Hampshire, Fred Astaire, Dustin Hoffman, Keira Knightley, Jay Leno, River Phoenix, Ben Elton, Sylvester Stallone, Billy Bob Thornton, Ruby Wax, James Whale, Robin Williams, Henry Winkler, Keanu Reeves.

Chefs

Jamie Oliver, Marco Pierre White, Rick Stein, James Martin.

Artists, Designers & Architects

Tommy Hilfiger, Simon Menzies, Andy Warhol, Mark Wilkinson, David Bailey, Lord Richard Rogers, Leonardo da Vinci, Pablo Picasso, Auguste Rodin.

Sportsmen

Muhammad Ali, Sir Jackie Stewart, Magic Johnson, Sir Steve Redgrave, Duncan Goodhew, Nola Ryan, Johnny Herbert, Sandy Lyle, Carl Lewis.

Inventors & Scientists

Alexander Graham Bell, Wilbur and Orville Wright, Albert Einstein, Sir Isaac Newton, Thomas Edison, Michael Faraday, Henry Ford.

Business Leaders & Entrepreneurs

Sir Richard Branson, Bill Gates, F.W. Woolworth, Peter Stringfellow.

Film Makers & Directors

Walt Disney, Lynda La Plante, Guy Richie, Steven Spielberg, Quentin Tarantino.

Composers, Musicians & Vocalists

Beethoven, Mozart, Robbie Williams, Damon Albarn, John Lennon, Brad Little, Noel Gallagher, Nigel Kennedy, Cher, Toyah Wilcox.

Political & Military Leaders

Winston Churchill, George Washington, Dwight Eisenhower, George Bush, George W Bush, John F. Kennedy, Michael Heseltine, Nelson Rockefeller.

Writers

Hans Christian Andersen, Agatha Christie, Benjamin Zephaniah.

SOME REVIEWS FROM OUR WEBSITE www.yeswecanread.co.uk

"There are so many people out there who can't read and need help - so why don't people who can read help people who can't?"
Sue Torr MBE, Literacy campaigner and author of *Secrets*

"Every time we turn a page, I understand more about the genius of *Yes we can read*. The big plus is that it makes learning to read fun."
Julie Carthy, Adult Education Tutor and Volunteer Reading Organiser

"I used *Yes we can read* with a child who had been receiving one-to-one help for 7 years and had reached a reading age of 5.5. After 10 weeks additional help using *Yes we can read* he'd made 18 months progress."
Geof Sewell, Teacher & University Lecturer in Special Needs

"If you know someone who finds reading difficult and learning to read didn't quite work the first time for whatever reason then this is the scheme for them: *Yes we can read* is just the magic you need to succeed."
Damien Jordan, Headteacher, Fairlight Primary and Nursery School

"I just wish they'd had *Yes we can read* when I was at school. Now I have learned to read and I am teaching my niece with *Yes we can read*. She is doing so much better at school, and her behaviour has improved too. I love reading bed-time stories with my son."
Catherine, young mother

"*Yes we can read* is amazing. It works, it absolutely works! You take a tadpole and watch the metamorphosis into a frog with little steps, slowly but surely."
Marc Wood, Step By Step Project Lead Tutor, The Friends Centre

"The layout is simple yet effective. The notes for the coach are clear and precise. The repetitive text enabled my reader to fully grasp the sound we were focusing on. The text is humorous and, at times, we would laugh out loud... Definitely a ten out of ten for it!"
Lisa Dickinson and Hayley Dawkins, Learning Assistants - joint coaches

"Patrick is 72 and the phonic alphabet is a revelation to him. He loves *Yes we can read* and described it as *his bible*."
Volunteer Reading Tutor

"When I came out of the library after teaching my learner, Moon Lim, my heart sang. She was a joy to teach and I feel like I gave her a real treasure."
Linda Curtis, Coach
Linda (67) went on to run We Can Read in Gosport and her learner, Moon Lim Englefield (65), became the NIACE South-East Adult Learner of the Year.

"I taught my dad to read when I was eleven. Sometimes it was tough but we had a good laugh as well. We are both well chuffed with ourselves."
Callum Morgan (14), Coach

"I learned to read with *Yes we can read* in our school reading club, where the Year 11s teach us Year 7s to read first thing in the morning. I finished the book just before half-term. I missed being part of the club, so I just went back again on the first day back. Now I am teaching my best mate to read with *Yes we can read*. It's me doing the coaching! I can read the coach instructions, because I can read what I want to now."
Leon Underwood (11), Year 7 pupil, Brune Park Community School

"Our *Yes we can read* project is here to stay. The results are extraordinary - for learners and for our coaches as well - and I have a queue of Year 10 and 11 students who want to teach reading."
Mikaela Milne, English teacher, Brune Park School

"Michael was learning from page one and he engaged with the book straight away. At the end of the session he said that he had enjoyed it and he had butterflies in his stomach because he was excited about the next session. I found the material very user friendly and the session as enjoyable as Michael did. Several of our learners from the hostels have finally been able to go to Alcoholics or Narcotics Anonymous meetings, as they can now read the Twelve Steps."
Rob Frier, Westminster Rough Sleepers Hostel

"I tried to learn to read lots of times, with all different teachers, but I never thought I would ever do it. When my coach sent me a postcard with lots of writing, I knew I had got it. I am 64 and I can read after all!"
Maureen

"People who are thinking about becoming or who are training to be a teacher will gain great confidence and satisfaction from the one-to-one coaching in *Yes we can read*."
Marcus Wright, Senior Maths Teacher, Cardinal Newman School

"*Yes we can read* is a very useful tool to engage and motivate young people and adults into developing their reading skills in a supportive way."
Vicky Duckworth, Senior Lecturer, Edge Hill University

"*Yes we can read* has enabled women readers to coach others, without the need for training, and allows the new reader to continue after release. This is a most powerful tool that encourages desistance from offending and is key to all prison Governors' aims."
Julia Killick, Governor of HMP Holloway

"The pattern repetition in sentences is very clever. It gives the reader the opportunity to read fluently and confidently early in the learning journey."
Adult Education Tutor

Why it works
It works because one-to-one is the way we learn to read.

Each photographed object is the same shape as its corresponding letter, removing a big hurdle for the learner.
Photographs are used because many people with dyslexia see letters as 3-dimensional objects.
Starting with this simple method for learning the sounds of individual letters (phonics) the learner will discover how to blend these sounds together, soon articulating whole words. Those words which don't follow the rules are learned in groups of *Look Write Say* words.
The reading adventure is broken into tiny steps, encouraging the learner from the outset with regular small successes. Each successful step is awarded a tick, building the learner's confidence as well as enabling the coach to identify where a reading problem lies.

The coach is shown how to overcome problems and turn any small difficulty into an opportunity for fun and shared games.

The learner's fear of long words is removed through word sums and by a very simple method of breaking words into syllables, covering them up and revealing each word-part bit by bit.

The reading material is designed to be fun, so the learner will soon develop the habit of reading for meaning.

Notes:

Sea Fever by John Masefield. From SALT-WATER POEMS AND BALLADS, by John Masefield, published by the Macmillan Co., NY, © 1913, p. 55; the poem was first published in SALT-WATER BALLADS, © 1902.